vision of a path to wholeness and unity in God's Spirit through understanding His true plan to express Himself uniquely through His ever-diverse creation "from every tongue, tribe and people" of a new nation, distinct in its parts yet appreciative of each.

And Randy gives us more than mere vision; he lays out practical steps to help us reach diversity without division, reconciliation without recrimination, restitution without retribution—all in the healing Spirit of Christ's love! I pray that Randy's work will move the hearts of millions as a restorer of a godly dream and a "repairer of the breach" in our (and the entire world's) torn and tormented social fabric.

Tony Marco, author, civil rights activist

A powerful, honest Native American voice articulating a multicultural, contextualized, thoroughly biblical Gospel. If from the beginning Euro-Americans had lived out this biblical vision, we would have avoided most of the terrible injustices of North American history.

Ronald J. Sider
Professor of Theology and Culture, Eastern Seminary
President, Evangelicals for Social Action

It refreshes me to hear the voice of the Native American and listen to his pain. Randy Woodley's voice comes out of an authentic Christian experience, not necessarily the European expression of Christianity. His God is a missionary God who speaks throughout the world and asks us to carry the good news of great joy to all men and women everywhere. I endorse this book wholeheartedly.

John Perkins, Founder
John Perkins Foundation
Chairman, Christian Community Development Association

This is perhaps the most important book any American citizen could possibly read who wants to truly understand global missions. Why? If we can't understand what we (mainly) did wrong with the "First Americans," how can we intelligently reach the world farther away? This book illuminates that embarrassing question with gentle fairness and profound insight.

Ralph D. Winter
Founder, U.S. Center for World Mission
General Director, Frontier Mission Fellowship

Randy Woodley has taken a complicated and sensitive subject and presented it in a simple and enjoyable way. He does this by using the gift of the Indian—getting to the point of the matter with humor, stories and humility. A must-read for anyone who desires to share Jesus cross-culturally.

Daniel Kikawa
Founder, Aloha Ke Akua Ministries

I found *Living in Color* intriguing for two reasons. First, as members of the Wind clan of the Creek Indian Nation, my family has shared experiences similar to those reported in Randy Woodley's book. As I read *Living in Color*, I discovered fresh aspects of my heritage that reminded me of my own multicultural history. I am delighted to see a book written from the perspective of Native Americans.

But second, one of the most urgent issues facing biblical church growth in North America revolves around multi-ethnic churches: churches transitioning into multi-ethnicity, churches carrying out multi-ethnic ministries, the intentional planting of multi-ethnic churches. While the idea of multi-ethnic ministry sounds appealing, the process is challenging.

Written by a Keetoowah Cherokee Indian, *Living in Color* is dynamic, thoughtful and pointed. You may not agree with everything Randy Woodley writes, but I know you will think deeply about multicultural ministry. Be prepared to feel a little uncomfortable, but most of all, be prepared to follow the insights suggested in the book to help build churches unified around the Lord Jesus Christ.

Gary L. McIntosh, Professor of Christian Ministry and Leadership
Talbot School of Theology, Biola University

Living in Color is a dynamic and insightful message that the Church today needs to hear. I believe that Randy Woodley has done no less in these pages than pen the heart of the Father. The Body of Christ is like a jigsaw puzzle, each piece unique and beautiful—yet only when each piece is interlocked with the others does God's true picture of the Church emerge. Through the pages of this book, Randy has brought that picture to light so that all who read it can catch a fresh vision of the Body of Christ, the way the Father intended it to be.

Richard Pyle, pastor, Tribe of Christ Church

What Leaders Are Saying About *Living in Color*

Living in Color strikes a chord that should resonate in the spirit of every believer, to love and appreciate one another in the midst of the amazing diversity that is the Body of Christ. How appropriate that a Native American, standing under centuries of injustice and rejection, would be one that almighty God would raise up to call us to embrace a view of the Kingdom in which every person is regarded with equal value and importance. I am grateful for this honest, sensitive and respectful portrayal of Native people. It serves to help tear down the negative stereotypes of Native people and reveal that all of us must own all of American history, if true reconciliation is to come to our nation.

Randy has been my friend and covenant brother for several years, and I consider it an honor to highly recommend his latest book to you.

Richard Twiss, President
Wiconi International

For too long our perceptions as Christians have been contaminated by our cultural bias. How can we grow from societal boundaries to possessing the mind of Christ, who values other cultures so much that He left heaven to be found in appearance as a man? Randy Woodley tackles this problem with Kingdom vision and with grace and truth.

Francis Frangipane, pastor and author

This book resounds with God's love for all the peoples He has made in His image. Through the stories of his own Native American heritage and the experiences of others, Randy Woodley develops biblical themes of justice, creation and God's love, along with biblical models of contextualization and diversity. This book will interest all those committed to racial and cultural reconciliation.

Craig Keener, author, IVP Bible Background Commentary: New Testament
and co-author, Black Man's Religion

Randy Woodley's book *Living in Color* is the most moving and riveting book we've ever read on the subject. He moved us to tears, laughter, contemplation, repentance and hope for our future, all within the pages of this profound and provocative book. His writing is clear and concise. He is direct but compassionate. He faces history but his examples include the good and the bad. That is rare in these days. He is openly transparent but not in a trashy way. His insights are valuable and timely. His vision is powerful and his direction is set for exploring the horizons of multicultural partnerships with the Gospel. Randy can be trusted because his biblical foundations are solid.

Every move of God has cutting-edge apostolic people who walk the front lines for God. Randy and Edith are this way for the First Nations people of

North America. We are thankful for their efforts on behalf of all of us. Thank you (*quyana*) for this wonderful book.

Dr. Suuqiina and Qaumaniq Suuqiina
Inuit Ministry International

Randy Woodley is one of perhaps two dozen First Nations leaders God is raising up in the new millennium to proclaim the news: You can be fully Native and fully Christian all at once. As we white Christians accept this message, which still seems like news, we can begin for the first time to attain reconciliation between whites and Natives. White leaders can reach out to Native leaders like Randy, and Natives to whites, respecting each other's strengths and integrity.

With his depth of learning (I've seen his library!), lived pastoral experience and reputation for integrity in white-Native reconciliation, Randy is the right person to communicate this vision. This book conveys the love vision of God's heart as expressed through a Cherokee soul.

Douglas McMurry, pastor and author

Our loving Father God is answering His Son's prayer in John 17. Randy Woodley's fine and timely book clarifies for our minds and hearts that unity is not uniformity or conformity. Neither is it mere acceptance, condescension or tolerance. Unity is active celebration of diversity. Randy makes it clear that diversity in unity is God's plan; that diversity is not just happenstance but the very plan of God to bring forth the best in all of us as we share who we are with one another.

It is good to read the work of a man who knows that getting along is not compromise that reduces all to less, but the laying down of one life for one another within the cultural context of each, so that every man is appreciated, met and enabled to become his own glory in the kaleidoscope of beauty that God, who loves variety, is creating. What Randy teaches is vital if we are to reveal Jesus to the hungry and usher in the end times.

John and Paula Sandford
Co-founders, Elijah House International

This book is very much needed in our world today and a must-read. Randy states eloquently and clearly the truth behind each people group— that is, God created all of us to be different from one another, and diversity among people groups and their cultures is part of His creation and plan. To learn this is the first step toward *being* Jesus to other cultures and accepting how they worship Him within that culture.

Tom Freeman, Christ in the Great Basin

When I finished Randy Woodley's *Living in Color*, I wept with joy—for good reason. Having been drawn by Christ from the civil rights movement of the 1960s and early '70s, I was grieved to see that movement shatter into warring hordes of special interests alienating each another and "balkanizing" our land. But Randy Woodley here offers us a mighty, biblically based

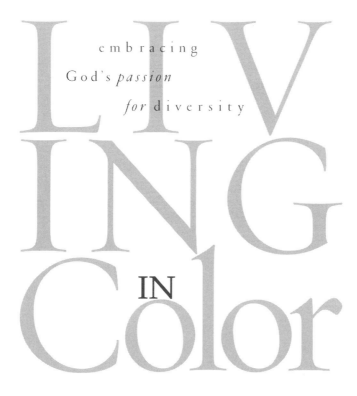

LIVING IN Color

embracing God's *passion* *for* diversity

foreword *by John Dawson*

RANDY WOODLEY

Chosen Books

A Division of Baker Book House Co
Grand Rapids, Michigan 49516

Published by Chosen Books
A division of Baker Book House Company
P.O. Box 6287, Grand Rapids, MI 49516-6287

Printed in the United States of America

Library of Congress Cataloging-in-Publication Data

Woodley, Randy, 1956–
    Living in color : embracing God's passion for diversity / Randy Woodley.
       p.   cm.
    Includes bibliographical references and index.
    ISBN 0-8007-9291-2 (pbk.)
    1. Christianity and culture. 2. Multiculturalism—Religious aspects—Christianity. I. Title.
BR115.C8 W 66 2001
261.8'34—dc21   2001028562

For current information about all releases from Baker Book House, visit our website:

http://www.bakerbooks.com

To my lovely wife, Edith;
my wonderful children,
Leanna, Skye, Young and Redbird;
and my gracious parents,
Ruben and Anne Woodley.
Thanks for putting up with the long hours
and short attention span.

Contents

Foreword

Living in Color is an excellent book, a readable adventure that touched my heart like few others. Written by one of the wisest, most trusted and fruitful Native American leaders of our generation, it leads us on a journey of discovery through the Scripture in order to see how God gives us identity in today's multicultural world.

This is an important book for all believers because the struggle to define identity affects all of us. It is an essential book, however, for indigenous peoples around the world, particularly the First Nations of North America.

Since Columbus made his journey west, new nations of refuge have emerged such as Argentina, Australia, Canada and Brazil. Most prominent among them is the United States. The experience of her Native peoples has become a pervasive part of global consciousness due to the dominance of American media. Does God have a unique purpose for indigenous North Americans? This book gives the answer in surprising ways. Sometimes controversial, sometimes provocative, but submitted in a spirit of humility and love, this is essential reading for anybody desiring to serve God's purposes in our generation.

As a person of European descent, I am profoundly aware of our tendency to quickly analyze what we see and start talking about it. At this point in history we will frustrate the gentle protocol of indigenous peoples and offend the Holy Spirit of God if we do not release our prejudices and suspend our presuppositions. In short, it is time to listen. As we do, I believe we will receive a great gift. This book is our opportunity.

Non-indigenous believers often express to me a fear of indigenous culture, associating it only with idolatry and occultic practices. There is some justification for this. The truth about Native beliefs and practices, however, is complex and varied. In some cases they have been shaped by a profound belief in a benevolent Creator. I believe it is the responsibility of indigenous believers themselves to separate the precious from the worthless in their cultures. Godly leaders like Randy know the Bible well and their cultures well.

This book clearly shows the difference between cultural relativism and moral relativism. It is not the form that is important, but the meaning attached to it. I have worked with Randy for many years, closely questioning the First Nations leaders with whom he works about their unique styles of worship. Instead of the syncretism I feared, I have seen an earnest insistence on the moral absolutes that flow from biblical revelation.

The personal struggle over identity that Randy Woodley reveals to us so honestly has resulted in a body of teaching that is highly relevant to Native and non-Native alike in our great urban centers. At a citywide Christian men's gathering recently in my native New Zealand, I gave a small talk on "Obtaining the Blessing—Giving the Gift of Identity to Our Children," and to my surprise received an overwhelming response from these largely European and Polynesian fathers. They yearned for an understanding of God's perspective on nationality, ethnicity, family destiny and personal gifting. These are truly universal concerns. I am grateful, therefore, to find that Randy provides a storehouse of wisdom for one of the great dilemmas of our time.

The more affluent a culture becomes, the more energy it invests in the search for identity. Once the issues of survival, shelter and the hope of a secure future have been addressed, a profound search for meaning begins, starting with the simple question "Who am I?"

Even nations struggle with the issue of identity. I met recently with concerned Christians working within the government of Singapore whose questions to me included "What are our gifts? How can Singapore serve surrounding nations? What national purpose do we suggest to our children as we prepare them for the future?"

How would you have answered them?

All nations and peoples are called to the dignity of leadership and all have unique personalities, but very few consciously apprehend that they possess gifts of service for other nations and people groups that are to be used under God. Could it be that the fivefold gifting mentioned in Ephesians 4 is not only a description of types of leadership in the Church but a reflection of a deep principle built into creation?

This book teaches us that, like the Trinity itself, we are a unity and a diversity, designed to serve and honor one another in relational oneness. That is the key to everything. The atonement mediated by Jesus at the cross has restored this potential to the human family. Let's live up to it!

If you want to know what that looks like in everyday practicality, read on.

John Dawson
Author, *Healing America's Wounds*
Founder, International Reconciliation Coalition
Los Angeles, April 2001

part 1

Understanding
Diversity

1

Uncovering the Myth
of Sameness

THE STORY IS TOLD of six blind men from Hindustan who tried to describe an elephant. The first said the elephant was like a wall, the next like a spear, another like a snake, then a tree, a fan and a rope. The lesson, of course, is that we cannot describe the nature of something merely by sensing one of its parts. We all see an elephant—or our small part of the world—from our own perspective. Yet there are many elephants out there, and it takes more than one viewpoint to appreciate them.

Surely this carries vast application to our understanding of the great God of the universe! We need a plethora of perspectives and cultural worldviews if we are to see a clearer picture of the immense grandeur of our Creator God.

I have been ministering among Native Americans for more than fifteen years, and have noticed a common occurrence when non-Indian visitors start to feel comfortable in one of our congregations. First they discover, to their great surprise, that the Native American people are "just like them." From their vantage point Indians live in the same kinds of houses, wear similar clothes and speak pretty much the same language. That is the honeymoon period. But invariably, within a few months, the honeymoon ends. Emotions surface, ranging from disillusionment to betrayal. I have actually heard people say, as they left a fellowship, "I thought I had a lot more in common with the people here, but they're just too Indian."

Too Indian, too black, too white—as if differences between themselves and others had suddenly appeared out of nowhere. The truth is, once we get close enough to any people group—or, for that matter, any person—we usually discover that many of our initial observations were based on false assumptions. Primarily we assume that everyone else in the world is "just like us." Why do we assume this? Foremost among many reasons, because we have not been taught to appreciate the diversity of other people and cultures.

The tendency to undervalue or devalue differing cultures and to expect sameness—a tendency prevalent in America—stems from the time our country was formed. When the first colonies were founded, rules were established that discouraged divergent views. For the first hundred years, for instance, Quakers and others who challenged the religious and social order in New England were dissuaded through violence, including hanging.[1] Other less "extreme" groups escaped with milder punishment, such as Baptists discouraged from divergent religious beliefs by public whippings.[2]

The American Indian culture suffered for its divergence as well. One of the systematic approaches to forcing sameness on Native Americans is considered the "elephant in the living room" to many in the Native community. This little-known chapter in United States history still affects many Indian families very deeply. Beginning about 1880 and lasting largely through World War II, thousands of Native children in the U.S. and Canada were manipulated or forced into leaving the security of their homes and families to attend government- and church-managed boarding schools. These institutions were run in strict military fashion and aimed at nothing less than turning every Indian child into a white Anglo-Saxon Protestant.[3] Many horrific stories surfaced later from those who attended these schools during a time when their motto was "kill the Indian, save the man."

One of the most poignant stories ever told to me about boarding schools involved a friend of mine, a Kiowa man who, by God's grace, later became a pastor. A missionary came to some of the Kiowas' homes in western Oklahoma when my friend was eight years old and basically "guilted" the parents into sending their children to the Riverside Indian Boarding School in Anadarko, Oklahoma. My friend's parents and some of his relatives sent a group of their sons with the missionaries who, working in conjunction with the federal government, had made this place sound special. The boys' parents and grandparents wanted them to appear their very best, so they arrived wearing their finest clothes and regalia, their long, dark hair neatly braided.

After arriving, the boys were stripped of all their clothes and regalia and assigned uniforms. They were deloused for good measure, and a bowl was put over each head as their long hair was cut off. (In Kiowa culture, as in most Indian cultures, cutting the hair is a sign of grieving or shame.) Finally they were directed to their new living quarters and sent to bed crying. The next day, Sunday, the boys were marched military-style to the chapel. Each in turn was shown a picture of Jesus and told of God's love for him.

Later that night the boys discussed this among themselves, whispering from their beds. What seemed so very strange to them was that for God to accept them, their hair had to be cut short; yet they had seen pictures with their own eyes that God's Son had long hair! It was a painful and confusing lesson.

Punishing others for cultural distinctives is by no means a solely Western European phenomenon. In most Native American tribes the name for *our own tribe* translates as "the people." My Cayuga friend Adrian Jacobs, a gifted teacher and director of First Nations Institute in Rapid City, says, "If we are *the people*, then what does that make everybody else?"[4] Ethnocentricity, such as is found in the name *We are the people*, indicates that we view anyone different as less than ourselves. At the most basic level our tendencies toward ethnic and cultural homogenization—trying to make others like us—reflect the fact that all cultures are sin-stained. As human beings we usually miss the mark of God's plan concerning unity in diversity.

19

Diversity from the Beginning

The tool of ethnic and cultural homogenization has been used throughout the centuries to protect what is valued in one's own culture. Usually this ethnocentrism stems from fear that differences will pollute the old way of life and the familiar standards of the culture.

On the one hand, the philosophy of homogenization makes perfect sense. Human beings naturally desire stability in life. Standards give us something to hold onto; they link us with the past. But God Himself wants to be the standard by which we measure everything in society. The difference seems indistinguishable unless we have a sound biblical and theological foundation that reflects God's true heart on any given matter.

To get a glimpse of the heart of God concerning diversity, let's consider the first example of diversified cultures presented in Scripture and see where God was heading at a time when everyone on earth had a common language and culture.

> They said, "Come, let us build ourselves a city, with a tower that reaches to the heavens, so that we may make a name for ourselves and not be scattered over the face of the whole earth." But the LORD came down to see the city and the tower that the men were building. The LORD said, "If as one people speaking the same language they have begun to do this, then nothing they plan to do will be impossible for them. Come, let us go down and confuse their language so they will not understand each other." So the LORD scattered them from there over all the earth, and they stopped building the city. That is why it was called Babel—because there the LORD confused the language of the whole world. From there the LORD scattered them over the face of the whole earth.
>
> Genesis 11:4–9

Although the Bible provides no physical descriptions telling us how one group of people differed from another, we can suppose that the seed for all the races were in Adam and Eve, and that people were, at least in some ways, different from each other. There seems to have been no inherent evil in having a culture of common language; rather, the people used this powerful communication tool in an evil way.

What was evil about this situation? The people's disobedience to God's commands. The people at Babel had one overriding motivation: to make a name for themselves. Their corporate self-admiration stood in direct contrast to the natural revelation of Himself that God had planted in their hearts, and it violated what would later be known as the first commandment. Think of what a tremendous ego boost it would be if everyone else were just like us! But trying to remake society in our own image would mean that society could not reflect God's image, for His image is reflected in the unity of our being like Him while at the same time being unique in ourselves.

The people's disobedience also stemmed from their resolve to remain in one geographical area. God's injunction from the beginning had been that people be fruitful and multiply and fill the earth. But the earth could not be filled when the people of the earth refused to leave its only city. God's command had never been withdrawn—it still has not, to my knowledge—and the people of Babel were in direct violation of it.

But let's think about God's strategy. Why would the Creator want them to occupy the ends of the earth, anyway? Didn't He realize that once they became separated by various geographical barriers, communication would be disrupted? Over time all languages naturally change. And people would eventually develop different physical characteristics according to the laws of genetics. Did God know what He was doing?

He did, indeed—and that is why acting in disobedience to His plan is just plain stupidity. God has planned since the beginning of time to cultivate diversity among human beings. When people tried to circumvent His plan, God intervened by creating many languages. Distinctions would have developed naturally over time, and changes would undoubtedly have taken place anyway if the people had spread out and obeyed God. His intervention merely sped up the process of developing the various ethnic groups that brought about His intended diversity.

The Scriptures do not say that the people of Babel looked much different from each other, but the laws of human genet-

21

ics show that after many generations, distinct physical genetic traits begin to repeat themselves in the same families. Nor would it have been beyond God's capability or design to have given certain families with genetic similarities the same languages when He separated them (for example, Oriental genetics and languages in contrast to Caucasian).

The Scripture notes that after God intervened, the people were scattered across the face of the earth and the city was never completed. This was a decided disciplinary action taken by the Creator to fulfill His original plan, but I would not call it a curse, as some have. If it was a curse, then it was a self-inflicted curse brought on by their stopping to build the tower, but out of God's discipline a great blessing was to be found in their inhabiting the whole earth.

God's plan of ethnic diversity is at least as old as the earth's first habitation. But regardless of human diversity, God always expects a unity of belief and obedience to Himself.

Can you imagine why the Creator intended such a wide diversity in people's cultures from the very beginning? Or why God's heart is turned toward our living in a multicultural world?

As I ponder these questions, I cannot help but realize that He is a God of innovation and extravagance, diversity and lavishness. God is the artist who formed the planet Saturn and its beautiful surrounding rings. He is the humorist who formed the giraffe and the narwhale, the armadillo and the platypus. God is the designer who set the constellations in place, who causes roses to bloom and who enables bees to make honey. We are not threatened by the stars that tower overhead or by a blooming rose or by the taste of honey in our tea. Should we be so surprised or threatened to find that God also created such diversity in human beings—all distinct and all equal—or that He insists that every culture be unique in its own right?

The Cost of Dehumanization

Colorado holds an annual celebration known as "Alfred T. Packer Day." To many Coloradans this day slips by without notice; most are ignorant of the history surrounding the occasion. Alfred T. Packer was a Colorado miner stranded in the mountains with his friends more than a hundred years ago. A blizzard set in and the four men found themselves at the brink of starvation. Only one man made it back to Denver that spring, and he was "looking more fit than he should."[5] From that point on Alfred T. Packer was less than affectionately known as "Cannibal Jack."

While human cannibalism must be one of the most dehumanizing acts possible, this story reminds me of hundreds of cases of *cultural* cannibalism. Both physical and cultural cannibalism begin with *condescension,* the notion that one person or culture has more of a right to exist than another, or than all others. This haughtiness of attitude assumes a superiority over the other person or culture. Thus begins the *dehumanization* stage, which can eventually lead to *calculated genocide,* as in the case of six million Jews under Hitler.

But genocide need not be carefully calculated to be effective. Consider the deliberate ethnocentrism that occurred in America after 1492. Sound estimates place the Indian population in the contiguous United States at the time of the arrival of Columbus at more than five million.[6] In 1900 the U.S. census recorded a mere 237,196 American Indians within her borders.[7] Although there has been no single policy spanning the past five-hundred-plus years, Native Americans have suffered genocide as a result of Euro-American ethnocentrism.

Here is the poignant observation of Tecumseh, the Shawnee chief who led a unified intertribal resistance against the Americans around 1810:

> Where today are the Pequot? Where are the Narragansett, the
> Mohican, Pokanoket, and many other once powerful tribes
> of our people? They have vanished before the avarice and the
> oppression of the White man, as snow before a summer sun.[8]

As the Creator has watched the decline of people groups and cultures, I wonder what His attitude has been. Could it be that each of these vanquished peoples held a special place in His heart? Perhaps each had a way of expressing themselves uniquely to the Creator. Perhaps it was in their name for God. Or perhaps His divine characteristics were retold in

23

ceremonies or stories that recalled His divine intervention. We will never know, unless it is through the conjecture of the archeologists and anthropologists, for many people groups and cultures have disappeared, and science does not usually deal in matters of the heart.

Call it dehumanization, ethnocentrism, racial homogenization or cultural cannibalism—when one culture begins to lift itself up as better than another and it has the power to do so, any inhuman act or deprivation can be, and has been, "justified." And when such atrocities take place, Satan has a field day.

Consider the politics of war. Having lived through several wars and having observed several other "near wars," I have noticed a pattern in the rhetoric that is meant to gear us up to being willing to kill "the other guys" without much regret. Words and stories are carefully chosen by the *spinmeisters* as they build the case against our neighbors. When the chosen enemy finally seems a little less than human, it is time to go in for the kill.

It amazes me to realize how far we have become removed from God's simple principles of unity within diversity! We forget that genocide and war are very personal matters, as expressed in a poem I wrote:

American Sons

At what cost, O God, has this country been born?
That of a fifteen-year-old Cherokee boy, Bird Clan, his father's
    only son,
protecting his country from tyranny?

At what cost, O God, has this country been born?
The blood of a young lad, MacNaughton, killed by the colonies'
    freedom-fighters
a world away from the heather?

At what cost, O God, has this country been born?
A mother's son of ten drumming for the corps? Cannons do not
    discriminate
by age or jacket color.

At what cost, O God, has this country been born?
Eighteen, hanging on a swampy cypress tree because of
    a glance
across the color line?

At what cost, O God, has this country been born?
Across salty seas, in a war to end all wars—the last man standing,
but barely a man, he fell.

At what cost, O God, has this country been born?
The Japanese took no prisoners. His last words,
the same spoken when he was two: "Mommy. . . ."

At what cost, O God, has this country been born?
Nineteen and frozen in Korea,
pneumonia kills a boy like a bayonet.

At what cost, O God, has this country been born?
Home from Vietnam but, once home, disappeared.
He saved the last bullet for himself.

Red . . . the land of the red man, barely visible, our red fading.
I see your red colors dripping, leaking, spewing, spilling,
Red from shame, red from anger—red on the land.

Blue . . . a young man waiting at Valley Forge, scraping frosty toes
    and seeing only blue.
Blue bodies in criss-crossed angles lying in a Wounded Knee ditch.
War mothers live a lifetime in blue.

And white? Not white that covers colors but white that heightens
    them;
pure, sacred, clean white, white for peace.
No white . . . none at all.

Mothers give birth to American sons.
Marching they go from womb to war.
Desperate grief cuts moms like a dull razor to the bone.

Fathers grieve, too, through thinly veiled rhetoric,
Recovering from lunacy—words that feebly justify
the death of "Daddy's boy."

White, there is little to speak of—just red and blue.
Greed, racism, control . . . evil triplets
overpopulating what still stands between America's shores.

At what cost, O God, has this country been born?
Surrender, yes, surrender—but a white flag to You, my Lord.
Not cowards but warriors who die in an instant and live forever
    heroes—
Birth us again, in white.

Randy Woodley, © 2000

Brothers, Neighbors

We can trace Satan's ethnocentric strategy even farther
back than Babel. Look at the account of Cain and Abel. Cain
wished to silence his brother's voice and stop his kind of worship because it was different from his own—and as a result
Cain slew his brother. The classic wrong answer came back
to God as Cain's immortal words resonating through the ages:
"Am I my brother's keeper?"

As my friend Robert Francis, the catalytic consultant for
the Indian Fellowships of Missouri and Arkansas, says,
"Cain's answer was not even worth a response from the Creator." Robert makes the point that being a *keeper* implies
control or paternalism. We are not our brother's *keeper*, he
says, but our brother's *brother*. This means we have even
more responsibility to our neighbors.

Indeed, we are our brother's brother. And, as Jesus pointed
out to the ethnocentric lawyer in the story of the Good
Samaritan, since everyone is our neighbor, we have an unde-
niable responsibility of love toward him or her. Put yourself
into the story:

> "A man was going down from Jerusalem to Jericho, when
> he fell into the hands of robbers. They stripped him of his
> clothes, beat him and went away, leaving him half dead. A
> priest happened to be going down the same road, and when
> he saw the man, he passed by on the other side. So too, a
> Levite, when he came to the place and saw him, passed by on
> the other side. But a Samaritan, as he traveled, came where
> the man was; and when he saw him, he took pity on him. He

went to him and bandaged his wounds, pouring on oil and wine. Then he put the man on his own donkey, took him to an inn and took care of him. The next day he took out two silver coins and gave them to the innkeeper. 'Look after him,' he said, 'and when I return, I will reimburse you for any extra expense you may have.'

"Which of these three do you think was a neighbor to the man who fell into the hands of robbers?" The expert in the law replied, "The one who had mercy on him." Jesus told him, "Go and do likewise."

Luke 10:30–37

Several points stand out immediately concerning our responsibility to our neighbor. First of all, recall that the expert in the law with whom Jesus was speaking was trying to *limit* the scope of his responsibility to others; hence Luke's phrase in verse 29: "He wanted to justify himself." Jesus' poignant story went to the heart of the matter. The lawyer would have excused the priest and Levite on reasons of blood defilement, but he recognized the moral dilemma Jesus was presenting. The very people the lawyer felt justified in disenfranchising—namely, the Samaritans, whose race and culture were an affront to the Jews—were the ones Jesus used to reveal the lawyer's twisted thinking and show God's heart on the matter.

In the end, just as God refused to answer Cain's ridiculous suppositional question, Jesus likewise did not answer the lawyer's question of "Who is my neighbor?" Instead Jesus forced the lawyer to pick the Samaritan—over two religious Jews!—as the person God wanted him to imitate. How that must have stung! The obvious lesson: We have a responsibility to *all* people, not just those who are like us.

The Bigger Picture

Perhaps the next logical question should be this: *Do I have a responsibility for my brother's culture?* It is one thing to tolerate another person's culture; and many people will come to the aid of a person in need, regardless of culture. Yet it is quite another thing to realize that if we do not protect our neigh-

27

bor's culture, we are actually assisting in its (and his) destruction. Recall the poignant echo of Tecumseh we just heard.

Frankly, if you believe somehow that my culture is not as important as yours, then you also believe I am not as important as you, and you miss the point of Jesus' story. I wonder how God might respond to the question, *Do I have a responsibility for my brother's culture?*

Before you answer, think of this question in light of such cultural atrocities as the Holocaust; the massacre at Wounded Knee in 1890; or, even more recently, Kosovo. Pastor Martin Niemöller, the Berlin pastor who opposed Hitler in World War II, brings the point home in a famous statement that is attributed to him:

> First they came for the Communists, and I did not speak out, because I was not a Communist. Then they came for the Jews, but I did not speak out, because I was not a Jew. Then they came for the trade unionists, and I did not speak out, because I was not a trade unionist. Then they came for the Catholics, and I did not speak out, because I was not a Catholic. Then they came for me. And there was no one left to speak out for me.

We are all different, yet we are all neighbors—or, if you will, brothers and sisters with the same ancestry. In Acts 17:26–27 Paul notes:

> "From one man he made every nation of men, that they should inhabit the whole earth; and he determined the times set for them and the exact places where they should live. God did this so that men would seek him and perhaps reach out for him and find him, though he is not far from each one of us."

What possibly could have been God's reasoning behind this? After all, to scatter people all over the earth, make of them different races and then give them different languages and cultures is not the way one would normally go about communicating a central message. Wouldn't the best way for a lot of people to find God be to gather all in one place? That did not work at Babel because they were not looking past their own ethnocentric pride. It did work at Pentecost because God found His people in unity and blessed them with the fullness of His Holy Spirit.

In Jerusalem at Pentecost, thousands of people from many nations had gathered, and God gifted them with the ability to hear the Gospel message in their own languages—sort of the converse effect of Babel. Then these folks dispersed to the outermost regions of the known world of that day—this time with the Good News, helping to fulfill again God's original injunction to fill the earth.

Nevertheless, the question begs an answer: Why scatter the nations if God wanted them all to hear the same message and to worship the same God?

We All Need Each Other

Could it be that the Creator made all the diverse ethnic groups so they would look to Him not only through their own eyes but the eyes of those different from themselves, so they might see Him more clearly? Perhaps through many perspectives, people would then cherish His vastness and His purposes for unity within His great diversity. The "bigness" of God has something to do with how we perceive Him in our own diverse cultures. One of the concluding scenes of history describes the four living creatures and 24 elders singing to the Lamb:

> "You were slain, and with your blood you purchased men for God from every tribe and language and people and nation. You have made them to be a kingdom and priests to serve our God, and they will reign on the earth." . . . Then I heard every creature in heaven and on earth and under the earth and on the sea, and all that is in them, singing: "To him who sits on the throne and to the Lamb be praise and honor and glory and power, for ever and ever!"
>
> Revelation 5:9–10, 13

Each people group possesses unique understanding and giftings that God has placed within that culture. Someone has said, "The whole council of God is found in the whole

Body of Christ." But each people group also wears cultural blinders. No individual alone, and no people group alone, can fully understand God. But working together, uniting our many different experiences, cultures and understandings, we can see more of the greatness of God.

This concept can be threatening to those who feel they need to control things and who must maintain a rigorous superiority to others. Yet I am pretty sure that God can handle all this diversity, and that He enjoys the many and varying ways we relate to Him and express our devotion.

Just as no one person has a "universal" voice pattern, retinal design or set of fingerprints, no one culture has the "correct" view of God. Since the Creator has gone to great lengths to create and establish a distinct "DNA pattern" for every culture throughout the world, with no two identical, shouldn't we in the Church set about the task of finding out why this diversity is so precious to the heart of God?

Our Ethnocentric Reality

To date our record is nothing to boast about. Sunday morning at 11:00 A.M. is still known as "the most segregated hour in America." Today's most popular church growth programs have planned homogeneity as their base formula. The fastest way to build a megachurch is to target one ethnicity, race, culture or income. The underlying assumption is that people enjoy their brothers and sisters in Christ more when they are just like them; it is more comfortable that way. Yet I cannot recall Jesus ever calling us to build our faith on comfort. Ultimately, on top of such a twisted theological base, Americans may have succumbed to the greatest temptation of all: to recreate God in our own image.

A recent news brief mentioned a pastor who refused to marry an interracial couple. Initially, when they had spoken over the telephone, he agreed to marry them, but he canceled the wedding after discovering that the bride was white and the groom was black. Apparently the pastor made his decision based on his belief that the Bible spoke against interracial marriage.

The state of Alabama, my own birth state, was the last state in the U.S. to repeal a ban on interracial marriage. In November 2000 the second amendment to the 1901 Alabama constitution was finally voted out. But the election results revealed that four out of ten Alabamans still believe it should be illegal for couples from different races to intermarry.

When I think about the pastor in the news report, and many others who hold similar beliefs, I wonder what he would do on Sunday morning if that same interracial couple showed up for Sunday school? My own mother-in-law, whose bloodline is half white and half Choctaw Indian, decided to try a new church in her own denomination. But Mom was asked politely to wait outside the church door until the pastor was summoned. The pastor met her at the door and informed her that she would be "more comfortable" at the Indian church on the reservation—which, unknown to him, she had been attending for years.

Not a solitary example, I am sorry to say. During a recent television interview with the pastor of one of the country's largest churches, the reporter noted that this huge church was composed of all white people. Then he asked the pastor what he would do if a black or Latino family came to his church. The pastor's response was disturbingly simple. In essence he told the reporter that because "they" were used to a more "lively" service, he would kindly refer the family to a church down the street.

Where do such attitudes originate, and what has God tried to do to reverse the tide?

God's Plan for an American Pentecost

One of the most significant events in the twentieth century occurred in Southern California at a street in Los Angeles in 1906 with an African-American preacher named William J. Seymour. The son of former slaves, and given the prejudice of society at that time, Seymour seemed an unlikely candidate to bring the heavenly vision. But he was used by God to deliver the message of His intent for the whole nation. The result: one of the greatest and most visible outpourings of the Holy Spirit, which caused a baptism of love to fall on all people groups.

I believe the Azusa Street revival, birthed as it was interracially and interdenominationally, was, in part, God's attempt to give America another chance to lift the curse of racism and ethnocentrism from our land.

At that mission in Los Angeles, for the first time in the twentieth century—and perhaps ever—God manifested Himself in America with our own Pentecost. Not only were blacks, whites, Hispanics, Native Americans and Asians touched by the Azusa Street revival, but as word got out, the nations of the world came pouring into Southern California to see what God was doing there.

Walls of separation by race and class were broken down. Years of hatred and bitterness began to be overcome, and America actually started to fulfill her destiny in God's wonderful plan of unity within diversity. This stood in startling contrast to the racism common at the time. It was especially notable that the Azusa Street integration occurred under the anointing of an African-American. It was obvious to most observers that God was sending a message to the Church and to the world expressing His own diverse character of unity in diversity.

During its initial two-year surge, it was common for the Azusa revival to hold meetings from early morning till midnight. By 1908 hundreds of ministries had been formed around the world as a result of the thousands touched by the Holy Spirit at Azusa. In May 1908 *The Apostolic Faith* newspaper reported the following spin-off, under the heading "Italians and Indians Receive the Holy Ghost":

> Truly the latter rain appears to be falling on every kindred, tongue and nation. While I was away, a number of Indians from the reserve, about 200 miles north, heard of the work in Winnipeg and came in the city. Five of them received the baptism and others were saved and sanctified. Since they returned home, we have heard that other Indians have been saved. While the Indians were at the meetings in the city, two of the Saints, under the power of the Spirit, spoke in other languages, which were understood by the Indians and one of the interpretations was, "Jesus is coming soon."[9]

But something insidious happened in Los Angeles, today one of the most multicultural and troubled cities in the world, following that blessed beginning at 312 Azusa Street.

The Reverend Mr. Charles Fox Parham, in many ways the catalyst and leading Anglo figure in this revival, would not tolerate what he saw occurring at Azusa. Parham, a known supporter of the Ku Klux Klan[10] who viewed "race mixing as the great sin of America," could not bear to see it at Azusa.[11]

We find differing viewpoints from various quarters as to why the Azusa Street revival eventually waned and died, but I believe Charles Parham's condemnation of the mixing of the races struck a blow deep to the heart of God and grieved the Holy Spirit.

Most of the Pentecostal denominations formed only a few years later had their roots in Azusa Street. Unfortunately these were not the earlier roots of brotherly love, creating a multiracial, multicultural Church standing as a prophetic call to the nation. Rather, division created denominations divided along the color line[12] and whose litmus test became "speaking in tongues as evidence of the baptism of the Holy Spirit." The fruit of the Spirit—which included the healing of the nations, or ethnic groups—was rejected. The religious leaders who first condoned and promoted the move of God at Azusa Street later condemned it, mainly because of the "mixing of the races."

This was Satan's divisive work. Similarly, some of the first colonists who landed on America's shores declared prophetically that they would be "a light to the nations and a city set on a hill." Unfortunately that declaration was soon forgotten, and religious and racial intolerance became pervasive. In 1906 America was still sore from the wounds of the Civil War, and Satan was thirsting for new approaches to keep minority groups oppressed—approaches like the Jim Crow laws from the 1880s to the 1960s, barring African-Americans from access to employment and to public places like restaurants, hotels, even bathrooms and water fountains.

God was looking for men and women to move in the opposite spirit from the racist spirit of the world. In the end, however, the philosophy of the world infected the Church, and new religious terms and doctrines were propagated that continued to spread the same old lies.

How could we have so missed God's plan for an American Pentecost?

> Utterly amazed, they asked: "Are not all these men who are speaking Galileans? Then how is it that each of us hears them in his own native language? Parthians, Medes and Elamites; residents of Mesopotamia, Judea and Cappadocia, Pontus and Asia, Phrygia and Pamphylia, Egypt and the parts of Libya near Cyrene; visitors from Rome (both Jews and converts to Judaism); Cretans and Arabs—we hear them declaring the wonders of God in our own tongues!"
>
> Acts 2:7–11

Like the original Pentecost, a wide diversity of people was present at Azusa Street to receive the blessing of unity. But the Church was simply not ready to see God's heart and follow His intentions. And to this day American Christians have not yet laid claim to the true inheritance God intends. His heart is still heaving with pain over the Church He loves deeply that continues to ignore His plan for her.

How can we sit comfortably in homogeneous services that differ so vastly from the intention of our Founder and not be embarrassed? Like Esau, we have sold our God-given birthright of the blessing of diversity for a mess of bland church stew. This stew will not fill our deepest hunger, nor will those homogeneous services help us become the diverse Bride of Christ that God has in mind.

I am grateful for Revelation 7:9, along with many other passages, that compel us to reject the myth of sameness and help us picture the Church God has planned in America and all over the world:

> After this I looked and there before me was a great multitude that no one could count, from every nation, tribe, people and language, standing before the throne and in front of the Lamb. They were wearing white robes and were holding palm branches in their hands.

In the Lord's Prayer Jesus prayed that God's will be done "on earth as it is in heaven." In heaven we see all the nations of the earth worshiping God together and singing a new song. Can you imagine it? Germans will be there with the French, Maoris with the British, Native Americans and Scots together, Australian Aboriginals, Saami, Hmong, Zulu and ever so many more, all worshiping Jesus in harmonious splendor.

God's new song cannot be sung solo. We all must sing it together, embracing and not restricting our diversity. May Your Kingdom come, Lord, on earth!

2

The Origins of Unity in Diversity

I ENJOYED THE STORY of a pastor trying to get his congregation to think in context with him. He would make a statement and they would respond. It went something like this:

Pastor: "Today we're gonna talk about something that happened waaaay back in the old days."
Congregation: "Go back, Pastor."
Pastor: "I'm talking back before the apostle Paul."
Congregation: "Keep going, Pastor."
Pastor: "I'm saying this was before Jesus Christ came to earth."
Congregation: "Go, Pastor, go back."
Pastor: "This was back before Isaiah, Jeremiah and Ezekiel."
Congregation: "Keep on going, Pastor."
Pastor: "Before Elijah and Elisha."
Congregation: "Keep on going, Pastor."
Pastor: "Even back before Abraham, Isaac and Jacob."
Congregation: "Keep going, Pastor."
Pastor: "Why, this was so far back, it was even before Adam and Eve in the Garden."
Congregation: "Keep going, Pastor."

The preacher in his enthusiasm really got going. He was on a roll and the people were right there with him.

Pastor: "I'm telling you, this was soooo far back, it was even before God!"

The congregation suddenly got quiet. The pastor, not quite realizing what he had said, was bewildered at their silence. Finally an older woman in the congregation spoke up.

"Pastor, if you want *me* to go with you, you'd better come back this way a little bit!"

Even though we are not going back quite that far, I want to ask you a question: What was God like before He created anything? Think about it. What was God like before the earth and sky were formed? Was He lonely, or was it enough for Him to be God, and He was, therefore, satisfied? Was God bored?

Since He was the only Being present, boredom would have been a reflection of His own nature—and even a casual observer can see by God's creation that He is definitely not boring!

No, most of us believe God was complete in and of Himself. He has never needed anything or anyone—and this is one reason life is such a great gift. Our lives were given to us not out of God's need for fulfillment, and certainly not from His expectation of repayment, but rather out of the magnanimous heart of a loving Creator. Everything we have is a gift, including diversity—because that reflects His own nature.

It was God's intention that human beings be diverse just as He Himself is diverse. In what way is He "diverse"? In His very own nature as the triune God—the subject we will explore in this chapter. God has always intended a single and unified purpose for everything that exists, just as He Himself, although three in Person, is in perfect unity. The reflection in human beings of both unity and diversity is part of what it means for us to be created in the image of God.

Before we look at the challenging concept of the diversity of our triune God, let us take a moment to appreciate His work in the world around us. In the middle of all the seemingly random things we observe every day, we can also observe a deliberate unity.

Unity in Diversity

Fall has always been my favorite time of the year. In Michigan, where I grew up, the hot summer is slowly swept away by autumn's cool breezes. Soft, green grass is covered by dying leaves, and the squirrels initiate their arduous nut-hiding maneuvers. Eventually fall turns to winter, and every creature, it seems, either retires or initiates a more cautious lifestyle. Then newborn creatures, along with the flowers of spring, arrive after the fresh new rains that melt the snows. All is dried by the hot breath of summer, only to be followed by autumn once again. It has been this way since the dawn of creation. God has made it so.

The great Creator has gifted us with unified but diverse patterns all around. Trees, birds, animals, even humans change their activities and "moods" during the different seasons. Even the most extreme or temperate climates have some change of season. Imagine a world where there was no seasonal change at all. Certain flowers would never bloom. Apples would never ripen. And in perpetual summer we might eventually get tired of all those butterflies (though it is hard to imagine!). God has set us in a very diverse world—but it functions in perfect unity.

All clouds are easily identified as clouds, although no two are alike. Blackbirds look alike to us, yet no two have ever been identical. Every wave crashes onto the shore with incredible repetition, but no two are just the same. This is true of every living thing that has ever existed—the same but different.

A seeming disruption in these patterns can be scary. The outbreak of a storm on a sunny summer day can be frightening, especially if you are caught outside without proper shelter. It is the extreme "differentness" of a thunderstorm that scares us. We hardly know what to expect. Will the lightning strike nearby? Will there be a tornado? Flooding?

The unity in the situation is that we know storms sometimes come and that they will eventually end. But it would be foolish for us to treat a severe storm casually; the consequences could be grave. So in some ways it is wise to be cautious when things are *too* different. Yet if we concentrate on the fear that the differences cause, we will never see their beauty. How beautiful are the lightning streaks that light up the sky! How pleasurable the scent of the air when the storm has lifted! What serenity in those last few drops as they spatter the ground and the storm ends!

Even our fear of difference is God-given. Although we reflect our Maker in many ways, He is still very different from us. We are created and He is not. To take His commands casually is the act of a fool. Proverbs 9:10 warns, "The fear of the LORD is the beginning of wisdom." Yet if we fear Him without trust, we will never come close enough to receive the great love He bestows so freely on us. The same is true of people. We must embrace our differences as opportunities to see them, and our world, in a new way.

The pattern of unity in diversity is not only natural but biblical. As it applies to our Creator's world, so it applies to our Creator.

The Blessed Three in One

Sometimes when I think about the Trinity, it blows my mind. I understand certain things about the concept, and I know most of the words theologians like to use to describe how the Father, Son and Holy Spirit are three in one. But it is an idea, like many truths about God, that boggles the mind. I have heard people say, "We'll understand it all when we get to heaven." Perhaps. But the Trinity is one of those concepts that may not be fully explainable.

Still, I have some thoughts about God that may be helpful in our discussion of unity in diversity.

First, we know that God is the only Being in this world who was not created. Every place, creature and person, by contrast, *has* been created. Human beings are unable to create something from nothing. Everything we "create" has been made from something else. The angels have no creative ability, nor does Satan; they, like us, are created beings. To create from nothing is solely the accomplishment of God.

We also know that the first pattern set in all living things is the pattern perpetuated. That is one reason evolution makes no sense. When a chicken lays an egg, both we and the chicken expect that, given the right circumstances for a healthy birth, a baby chick will eventually break through the shell. When an apple tree bears fruit, we expect that fruit to be apples. At human childbirth, a boy or girl is born and remains human throughout his or her life. The genetic pattern of an organism remains constant throughout its life.

These same principles apply to God. He intended it to be this way. All of creation bears His mark. And since He created us in His image, we carry God's particular "DNA." In what ways? In both unity and diversity.

The Bible explains the Almighty as God the Father, God the Son and God the Holy Spirit. A number of Scripture passages, such as Mark 1:10–11, use a Trinitarian formula, showing God in each of three Persons. The word *trinity* itself is just a shortened version of the words *tri-unity* or *unity of three*. Although it is not a biblical word (in that it does not appear in the Bible), *Trinity* and *triune* are perhaps the best words we have to describe God in His threefold nature. (A few other examples of the Trinity are found in the following passages: Matthew 28:18–20; Hebrews 10:29; 1 Peter 1:2; and Jude 20–21.)

Three people in unity is not a foreign concept to us. After all, we recall images like the Three Musketeers, who were different people but whose purpose was one. (The Three Stooges also worked toward the same goal; they just took longer getting there!) But the Father, Son and Holy Spirit are not simply three individual Persons; and they are certainly not three different gods with the same motivation, although they are sometimes misunderstood in this way. No, the Father, Son and Holy Spirit are one God—of the very same essence, if you will, and with the very same power and authority. God is truly the divine "three in One."

We have all heard the water, ice and steam illustration of the Trinity—different expressions but the same essence. Anyone who has seen hot springs in icy winter can relate to those three forms all together. But the concept of the Trinity became a lot clearer to me through another illustration one day when I was fishing at my wife's reservation on the Little Wind River in Wyoming. Standing in the cold, clear water, casting my line for a nice native trout but not catching much, I found myself staring down into the water.

All of a sudden I got it! In those cold waters I understood something about God I had not realized. I was standing in *one* river—the Little Wind—but the water that was flowing toward me, although it came from the same source, was not the very same water I was standing in. And the water passing me, out in the middle of the current, was not the same water I was standing in. It was all the same river, from the same source, but it was different water. The light went on!

That day on the Little Wind River, I began to see *with my heart* the imprint of God's unity in diversity all around me. I began to take notice of everything around me that bore God's triune design.

I recalled that familiar way to define a *man or woman:* body, soul and spirit. *Time* can be seen as past, present and future. The essence of the *family* is husband, wife, children. *Growth* can be seen as child, youth, adult. *Fire* equals coals, flame and smoke—all three necessary. The *earth* is dirt, rocks and grass; and the bigger picture—crust, magma and core. I realized that the Trinity design, God's unique DNA—unity in diversity—is everywhere.

Triune from the Beginning

Are you thinking that the Trinity is solely a New Testament concept that came into being with the advents of Jesus Christ and the Holy Spirit into human affairs? That is not the case. Marks of the triune God are prevalent in the Old Testament as well. God is called Father. Israel is known as God's son. The phrase *the Spirit of the LORD* is used liberally. In fact, the very first verse of Genesis marks God as triune.[1]

Genesis 1:1 states, "In the beginning God created the heavens and the earth." The Hebrew word for God, *Elohim,* is plural—but not plural in the sense of *gods created.* Nor is it plural in the sense of *Give me some grapes,* which would mean more than one grape. Rather, it is plural in the sense of *Give me a cluster of grapes.* A cluster is *one* cluster, full of *many* grapes. The word used here for *created* is singular, which denotes a single unity and purpose in the creation of the heavens and the earth.

41

In Genesis 1:26 God says, "Let *us* make man in *our* image, in *our* likeness" (emphasis added). Aren't the words *us* and *our* unusual choices? If God were one Person, He would have said, "*I* will make man in *My* own image, in *My* likeness." Since there was no one but the angels present, we might assume that God was speaking to them. But God was not speaking to the angels—for as we just stated, they have no creative ability and thus had no part in the creation. Besides, if God had been talking to the angels, the phrase *in our image, in our likeness* would presuppose that humans are also created in the image of angels, and this cannot be supported by the Scriptures.

This early stage in the book of Genesis does not reveal a great distinction between Father, Son and Holy Spirit, but the image of a plural unity is present nonetheless.

Later in the Scriptures God gives us a fuller understanding of the Trinity. Deuteronomy 6:4 states, "Hear, O Israel: The LORD our God, the LORD is one." Again, *one* is *Elohim*. In fact, *Elohim* is used thousands of times in the Old Testament to describe God. The word *El* can be attributed to God alone, yet it is used in reference to the Father in Genesis 14:18–22; to the Son in Isaiah 7:14; and to the Holy Spirit in Job 33:4.

Many other places in Scripture demonstrate this peculiar use of the Hebrew language to denote God's unity and diversity as we know it to exist in the Trinity. When the Scriptures are seen as a whole, these allusions to the Trinitarian nature of God make perfect sense. Nature around us (as I discovered during my unsuccessful fishing expedition) confirms this pattern. The Trinity may be beyond our comprehension, but as mere human beings we do not have the option of telling our Creator what His nature and essence should be. We do not completely understand because we are created beings and He is not. The Father is the uncreated God. The Son is the uncreated God. The Holy Spirit is the uncreated God. And the three are One.

God Wants a Community

So unity in diversity is part and parcel of who God is. His very nature is unity expressed through diversity. If God were not three in One, but rather one in One, He would seem to us to be an arbitrary dictator. If He were two in One, He would exist in a partner relationship with Himself. But God is three in One, and three is the first possibility for community to exist. The Father, Son and Holy Spirit, in and of themselves, make up a perfect community.

Recall the question I raised at the beginning of this chapter: Was God lonely before the earth and sky were formed, or was it enough for Him to be God, and He was, therefore, satisfied? We have seen that God, in His perfect diversity, enjoys perfect unity. We have also seen that He created a world according to His own DNA profile. Because diversity is found in the very nature of God, and consequently by design in us, we who are made uniquely in His image should not merely tolerate diversity in our own lives, but seek it and celebrate it.

And the only way to bring unity to diversity is a community of brothers and sisters devoted to God and living in obedience to Him.

There is no escape clause in God's design, since we are created to worship only Him.

The Lord has given us many community models to explore and enjoy that exhibit this unity in diversity. The first was in the Garden of Eden. Adam and Eve were one in community. But after our original parents sinned, the Bible says they hid from the Lord's presence. In essence they tried to shut God out, make a community of two and break up the community of Adam, Eve and their Creator that God intended. But two never make community; it takes three.

Our own sin will always break God's intentions for community. It took Jesus' sacrifice on the cross to restore the community God desires for humankind with Himself. That was the only time God stepped outside of His perfect community—when Jesus willingly became a human being. Note in Philippians 2:7–11 that it was because of our sin that the Trinity was disrupted. Our sin caused the Creator of the universe to abandon for a time the perfect model from which every other community derives its design and meaning.

When Jesus hung on the cross and asked the question, "My God, My God, why have You forsaken Me?" much more was at stake than His own abandonment. God was redefining the eternal order of community (as He had tried to do with Adam and Eve) by bringing human beings into a new relationship with Himself. Jesus, who walked as a Man in closer communion with God than any man had ever done, was asking, "Why have We, the Trinity, broken Our fellowship?" The beautiful oneness that had existed since before creation had now been severed. Why? Because God, the loving Creator, had given Jesus Christ, His only Son, as the perfect sacrifice for sin in order to restore mankind to Himself—to bring every human being who trusted Jesus back into His community.

The Scriptures are clear that God wants a people in communion with Him. This may be His foremost desire. God longed for Adam and Eve and their offspring to be in community with Him. He yearned after Israel like a faithful and devoted lover. And He is calling you and me to enjoy that special and most intimate kind of community. God enjoys our great diversity and delights in our unity. He wants everyone to be different and everyone to worship Him alone.

Choosing Jesus over Cultural Christianity

I WAS IN MY FIRST MONTH as a pastor in northern Nevada and was anxious to begin nurturing a Native church in the Indian community. It was at a pow wow (an Indian social dance) where I got my first resistance. As I talked to a woman who knew the history of our church, she commented, "No matter what you do from that church, Christianity will always be seen as the white man's religion."

Because my philosophy of ministry was (and still is) directed primarily toward Native Americans by Native Americans, using Native American cultural forms to witness for Jesus, this woman's observation hurt deep in my soul. Yet I have heard similar statements expressed for many years now. What did she mean?

First, let me discuss a few words. There are many ways to describe the indigenous (or original) peoples of North America. Today the most politically correct term seems to be *First Nations.* As you may remember, we used to be called American Indians and then Native Americans. The dilemma was, as the critics report, between honoring Columbus' mistaken "discovery" of India and Amerigo Vespucci's exploits. Besides, the Latin roots of *native* are the same as for the French term *naïve,* and even if we were back then, we certainly are not now!

While I do not want to offend anyone, I am comfortable using all these terms interchangeably; but most often, when I must use a name (other than my tribe) to describe myself, I say *Indian.* No, actually, I say it like this: "Indun."

I once heard a man for whom I have a great deal of respect, elder Jerry Yellowhawk, a Lakota (Sioux), address a crowd about this subject. He said that in his heart he would always be an Indian. I guess I feel the way Jerry described. I do not believe that more or less dignity comes from using one name over another. Our dignity is God-given, and I was raised to believe that *Indian* is a name to be proud of. Its roots may lie in the Latin phrase *en Deo,* meaning *in God.* I think that describes most of our people pretty well.

In any case, the woman at the pow wow was referring to the fact that for Native Americans to become Christians has often required us to divest ourselves of most of our cultural distinctives, including language, hairstyle, values and devotional practices. It is assumed that there is nothing in Native American culture worth redeeming. This evangelistic philosophy, brought over to the New World from Europe, made the broad assumption that European culture was "Christian" and that Indians needed to conform to Euro-American culture in order for God to accept them. R. Pierce Beaver, former professor of missions at the University of Chicago and director of the Overseas Ministries Study Center, summarizes the view of most missionaries in the eighteenth and nineteenth centuries, as well as in the first third of the twentieth century:

> Missionaries during this period believed that teaching primitive people about a "better" way of living was part of the Gospel message. Evangelization and civilization could not be separated. You could tell if an Indian was being saved from Hell by the way he or she began to live like the English. The Indians' growth in the Christian faith could be measured by how well they accepted the culture and lifestyle of the missionary.[1]

This European-ethnocentric model of evangelism has caused Jesus to be relegated, in the eyes of many indigenous

46

peoples, to one particular race. How this must grieve the heart of God!

My wife, Edith, and I worked very hard in Nevada under God's leading to build a Native church that reflected Christ in our culture. In many respects we were successful. But although we added many components of Native American culture to our worship services—including drums, talking circle, smoke blessing, sweat lodge and eagle feathers (all symbolic forms used in traditional Native American worship, which we felt had enough biblical backing to be used in the church)—it still did not always "feel" like a Native church. It was only in the last two years of pastoring in Nevada, I believe, that we became a church with which Native Americans readily identified. This transition took years to accomplish, and a relinquishment of power from a group of non-Indians.

After that non-Native group serving in leadership gave up their positions, the Indian people felt the freedom to be a church that reflected Christ in their culture. Soon afterward someone suggested rearranging the chairs in a circle. (Most of our traditions use a circle.) Then the style of governing changed to a more traditionally Native approach, and it grew from there. One day I realized we were no longer a church that did a lot of Native American things, but we were actually a Native church. Those were the years we had the greatest impact in the non-Christian Native community, and true discipleship took place. Why? Because we had finally allowed Jesus to be at home in our people's culture.

"Contextualizing" the Gospel—adapting the message to the culture of the people to whom you are seeking to witness—is not unique to the Native American situation. I have spoken with African-Americans, Asians and Hispanics who recount similar experiences. It is sometimes difficult for the average American, who identifies primarily with his Euro-American or Western European roots, to grasp the differences in the way he thinks, acts and believes from his brothers and sisters more oriented to another worldview.

When one culture is the standard by which everything else is measured, the people absorbed in that culture may not feel the need to consider other perspectives. This has been true for Euro-Americans for about five hundred years. But things are changing rapidly. Soon Euro-Americans will no longer be the majority ethnic group in the United States. (You might want to glance ahead to the statistics in chapter 7 in the section "What Does the Future Hold?") It behooves us as believers in Jesus to get a jump on the rest of the world in learning how to get along with each other and to appreciate our many differences, in order for Christ's witness to arise more effectively. Isn't action better than reaction?

Truth and Reality

While the percentages of minority groups in America are growing rapidly and the face of the nation is changing, almost every system is still dominated by Western European thinking. Consider learning styles. In America most children go to school for thirteen years and receive a diploma. The educational system is based largely on their ability to retain facts. It is largely a knowledge-based attainment. Many graduates go on to college and acquire more knowledge. Soon they declare a major and perhaps gain a bit of experience along with their knowledge, although that usually comes in the final year (if at all) or during the pursuit of a master's degree. If a person really wants to be considered an expert, he or she will go after a doctoral degree as well.

This system works well for most with a European worldview; it works less well for other groups, and not at all in Indian country. In the Native worldview a person who knows mostly theory is considered to know very little; and most of what means something to American Indians cannot be learned in books. What is more important to a group of Native Americans? Honesty, wisdom and experience. In Indian country true knowledge is not so much about facts as it is revelation from God.

I was taught by elders to observe closely when a task was being done and not to ask questions. After a while I was given the opportunity to try it, and I was corrected when I messed up. I was told to pray about these things and meditate on them. Every so often my questions—which were still in my heart and mind—would be answered. This learning style was very different from my training in college and seminary, where I was certified based on my knowledge of certain facts.

In the Indian world we *experience;* in the Euro-American world we *gather facts* about it. Someone has said that Native Americans would rather participate in a ceremony while Euro-Americans would generally rather read a book about it. Our concepts of time, material wealth and relationships (to name just three) are very different.

Another vast difference in cultural thinking between Euro-American and American Indians is found in our views of reality. The European influence of empiricism teaches Americans to question every fact in order to establish its *reality*—but not necessarily its *truth.* In Native American cultures, and other cultures as well, stories prevail. Euro-American society has labeled these "myths." But by *myths* they mean that not only are they not *true,* but they are not *real* either. The majority society also tells stories using its cultural symbols, but these are known as "fables." Although a fable can have a moral, it is still considered not real.

Here is an example. When I share Native American stories at elementary schools and churches, which often involve animals talking, I am interrupted spontaneously by Euro-American students challenging the reality of the stories. I do not blame them; they are just preserving a standard of their culture when they say, "Uh . . . animals can't talk." But to this day I have never had an Indian child dispute this dynamic of the stories. In fact, far from engendering skepticism, talking animals are more likely to connote a special sacredness. From a cultural standpoint Indian children are not concerned with whether or not a bear or rabbit or opossum can talk; they are listening attentively to what the animal has to say. In this sense Native youngsters are concerned about what is *true.* The question of what is *real* is not relevant.

Says Robert Antoine:

> Myths are not lies or secondhand "unscientific" approaches, but [an] . . . irreplaceable method of grasping truths which otherwise would remain closed to us. "The language of a myth

is the memory of a community," . . . which holds its bonds together because it is a "community of faith."[2]

The Bible tells of a donkey that talks, storms that listen, fish that swallow prophets and deliver coins. Is it possible that in these particular points of biblical interpretation, the simple Native American child has a perspective that could aid the earnest and listening European scholar?

Every culture has stories; recall Euro-American examples like George Washington and the cherry tree, and the first Thanksgiving. Whether or not the Pilgrims and Indians celebrated at Plymouth together as brothers is not as important to me as the sacred truth that the story delivers, challenging us to embrace each other as people different from one another and yet the same. This is worth the retelling of the story.

Every culture also has its myths, rituals and ceremony, although these are words that, to many Euro-American Protestants, have almost become sacrilegious. Still, Native rituals and ceremonies tend to draw us into an intimate association with past events.

> Ultimately, rituals bind the community together, and give it a sense of common identity by giving it a common fellowship and history. For example, it is interesting that American missionaries often celebrate the Fourth of July abroad as a way of reaffirming their American identity. Somehow if they do not do so, they feel less "American."[3]

Rituals and ceremonies are markers of remembrance for the things that mold us as a people.

When Jesus Enters a Culture

We readily observe numerous differences between people groups. Many of these are cultural and may not, from God's perspective, be right or wrong. We are just different. What *is* wrong is condemning another culture just because it is not like our own. Do you realize this has happened all over the world?

Many Jews continue to live their lives apart from Jesus Christ, their Messiah, because they have been persecuted over many centuries in His name, which has been used in defense even of the Holocaust. Then there are Muslims who may never come to Jesus Christ simply because of the self-righteous vigor that fueled the violence and murder during the Crusades. And for hundreds of years Christians have justified their oppression and near-extinction of American Indians in the name of Jesus. People usually do not purpose to spread an oppressive spirit; they acquire it over time by rationalizing their superiority and justifying lawless acts based on another group's supposed inferiority. It all begins with the notion that something (if not everything) about the other culture is wrong.

Sometimes God breaks through these steel walls of the past, however, and opens up a glorious light so that the Gospel may be seen clearly.

A few years ago a missionary to Bangladesh wanted to visit me. She was interested to note the parallels between my ministry among Native Americans and her own work among Muslims. My first thought was to discourage her from visiting, as I could not even begin to think of how our ministries could find any common ground. The only similarity I could think of was that both groups are nearly impossible to reach for Jesus!

I invited her to come anyway. As we shared our attempts to show Jesus to these two peoples in context, according to their own cultures, I was amazed at the parallels between our ministries. Not only were we both having some success where there had been little in the past, but these peoples were both taking responsibility for their growth in Christ.

The greatest similarity was in the issue of identity in Christ. Neither the Bangladeshi Muslims nor the traditional Native Americans identified themselves as "Christian." These were people who had been truly converted to Jesus Christ and were following Him daily; yet they chose not to use the term we bandy about today for things as trivial as fashion wear. These converts identified themselves as Muslim and Native American followers of Jesus, just as many Jewish believers in Jesus refer to themselves not as Christians but as "Messianic Jews." The Bangladeshis and Native Americans saw no value in attaching the old stigma to themselves that has brought so much pain to their people. Rather than embrace Christianity, they simply want to follow Jesus.

"I Ain't No Christian"

Early in my pastoral career I met a man who was very traditional in his Indian beliefs and practiced them daily. When we first met he vowed to me that he would never go inside a white man's church as long as he lived. I listened to his reasons (which had to do with Indian boarding schools) and told him I understood. Then I invited him to attend my sweat lodge—a cleansing, Native American–type sauna in which prayers are said. He was shocked that the new preacher "held sweat," but eventually, after I attended a few sweats with him at his home, he did come to my sweat lodge.

This exchange took place over a few years. I continued to pray for him. Finally one day he walked through the doors of the church. What he found was not a "white man's church" but a church of Native American believers following Jesus and using their own Native cultural expressions and symbolism. He began coming more frequently. After nearly five years I was able to introduce him personally to Jesus Christ.

Not long after my friend's conversion, I told a group of ministers gathered for prayer at our church about his decision to follow Jesus. By coincidence, about ten minutes later, my friend showed up at the church. Realizing who he was, one of the pastors jumped out of his chair and shook his hand, welcoming him to the Kingdom of God. He cried jubilantly, "I'm so glad to hear that you're now a Christian!"

My friend stepped back. "I ain't no Christian!" he exclaimed.

The pastors were stunned. They all looked at me as though to say, "Why did you tell us he was a Christian and he isn't?"

I kept silent.

Finally one of them spoke up. "Randy told us you had recently begun following Jesus."

"Oh, I see what you mean now," he said. "Yeah, I'm following Jesus Christ—He's Grandfather's Son—but I ain't no Christian. Don't call me that."[4]

He Invades Every Culture

According to a conversation I had with missiologist Ralph Winter, my friend was on solid biblical ground. Nowhere in the New Testament, Dr. Winter pointed out, does anyone ever call himself a Christian. Yes, believers were first called Christians at Antioch, but no one gave himself this title. Neither Paul nor Peter nor James nor anyone else ever identified himself as a Christian.

My point here is not to try to change people from calling themselves Christians. I have referred to myself as a Christian for more than 25 years. But we must realize that, to many people groups, the term *Christian* is not the good news we intend it to mean. Rather, it is the bad news of colonialism, oppression and even genocide. It is bad news because many of those who have named themselves after Christ have acted in very un-Christlike ways; and the cultural baggage that comes with the name *Christian* is sometimes unnecessary, and at other times actually *opposed* to Christ and His purposes.

My intention in this chapter, then, is to begin to evoke doubts about the "Christian-ness" of our own worldviews and cultures, regardless of what those may be. Don't you agree that Jesus invades everyone's comfortable culture like a whirlwind and starts blowing up dirt and rubble everywhere? If we take Him seriously, Christ calls us to examine everything in our culture, whether we consider it good or bad, and to turn it upside-down to see if it is aligned with His new Kingdom culture of righteousness.

It matters not if our culture is Euro-American, Native American, African-American, Asian-American, Latino or something else. When we become Christ's followers, all cultures are suspect, especially our own, and we must reexamine them in the light of God's Word.

Are you willing?

Biblical Faith and God-Given Culture

OUR SOCIETY IS NOT THE FIRST to tackle the issue of culture and faith—not by a long shot! Many examples in the Scriptures reveal ancient struggles people had with their ethnic identities, only to wind up finding God's true purpose for their lives and even for their whole generation.

Let's look briefly at three biblical examples: Moses, Esther and Paul. By being part of at least two different cultures, each was positioned to be used by God for His purposes.

The Egyptian Jew

Moses had no choice but to sort out issues of culture and faith; and through the struggle, God used His servant's unique bicultural situation to release a whole nation from slavery. Because we know the story so well, we usually forget some of the important cultural dynamics. Don't overlook the drama of Moses' identity issues.

Moses was born a Jew—although he did not know this as he grew up—and he was raised in the household of the Pharaoh, the leader of Egypt who held Moses' own people in slavery. Usually we move very quickly from *Moses the Egyptian* to *Moses the Jew*, yet imagine the trauma Moses must have gone through during the revelation of his true ethnic identity, which had been withheld from him until he was an adult.

Moses could easily have denied his own ethnicity and continued to live in the comfort of the king's palace, but he allowed God to use his once-hidden ethnicity in a powerful way. When he discovered his own Israelite heritage, he chose to identify with it. But culturally Moses was an Egyptian. Like all of us, he had to examine the culture in which he had grown up and decide what was godly in it and what was evil.

Even after his years with the Midianites (his father-in-law, remember, was a priest of Midian), and then his forty years with the Israelites, he likely always carried part of his Egyptian culture with him, even if it was only in his own thoughts.

My father-in-law was born a Shoshone on the Wind River Indian Reservation in Wyoming. As a child he spoke only the Shoshone language. At age eleven he was sent off to government Indian boarding school in South Dakota where, as he would say later, his teachers tried to "drive the language and culture out of me." My father-in-law continued to be a fluent Shoshone speaker throughout his life. Although he learned English and adapted to white society, he lived 71 years thinking like a Shoshone. In his last days on earth, he was heard many times by his family members speaking the old Shoshone language. In spite of boyhood beatings and other forms of humiliation, my father-in-law knew deep down that he was a Shoshone Indian.

The converse situation was true for Moses. He knew how to be an Egyptian; what he wanted to grasp was his birth identity. How often in his earlier years of pilgrimage would Moses have said to himself, *Think like a Hebrew!* Perhaps, living in the desert with the Midianites after he left Egypt, he would grow confused in ceremonies similar to ones he learned growing up in Egypt. Perhaps he found himself craving particular foods served to him in his childhood (as I do). Certainly he spoke and wrote in his native Egyptian language, which employed uniquely Egyptian concepts and symbols.

Moses was thoroughly a product of Egyptian culture, and I am certain the old adage (adjusted slightly) applied to him: *You can take the man out of Egypt but you can't take Egypt out of the man.*

Because of this cultural dissonance, living in two cultures different from the one in which he had grown up,

Moses had to make choices on how he related to the world. He could pick his clothes, language, foods and lifestyle. He could train himself to employ a new primary language. But his thought patterns and other innate distinctive Egyptian ethos would remain with him for many years, if not throughout his lifetime.

Americans, like Moses, also live amid many cultures. Few citizens are actually monocultural. Many distinctives set us apart that have to do with geography, ethnicity, political persuasion, financial status, religion and many other factors. Do you realize you make cultural choices on a daily basis?

This point was driven home to me on a recent trip to Calgary University in western Canada, where I noticed an inordinate number of women wearing traditional female Muslim dress—the flowing, full-length robe or *chador,* including the headpiece that covers all but the eyes. Then I overheard part of a conversation between two women draped from head to toe in this concealing attire, one of them of African heritage, the other most likely of European. As they discussed their choices to follow the teachings of Islam, one was chiding the other because of her inattention to certain cultural details. The other responded in frustration, "I don't know if I'm ever going to get this right."

It was obvious to me that these two women had chosen a culture foreign to them and were grasping somewhat clumsily for another culture, to the exclusion of their own God-given cultures.

Moses had a steep learning curve, too. The Israelite culture to which God had called him was foreign to this Egyptian prince, and it must have taken him a while to feel at home within it. At the same time, because God has been and is at work in every culture, using elements in them to point to Him, there are few cultures so corrupt as to have nothing godly in them, including Moses' Egyptian heritage. (Sodom and Gomorrah, however, would be two exceptions.)

So, was it inherently evil for Moses to allow some of his Egyptian-ness to come through? Not at all. God does not condemn us for embracing various elements of our cultures, but He does expect us to examine each element in light of His Kingdom values. Like Moses we are called to consider what is good or bad and discard the bad in favor of the Kingdom of God.

A Jewish Woman in the Culture of Persia

Queen Esther is another person who reclaimed her God-given culture. The beautiful woman whose Hebrew name was Hadassah willingly hid her Jewish cultural identity in order to live more easily among the Persians in King Xerxes' household. Her older cousin, Mordecai, who had brought her up, had asked her to keep her nationality a secret, knowing it could work against her. But at the right time, at Mordecai's advice, she revealed her ethnicity to the king and, as a result, saved her people from destruction.

When Esther revealed her Jewish identity, she did so at risk to her own life. The Jews had a minority standing in Persia at the time, with many enemies, and the king had already declared their projected demise. In the story we tend to recognize Esther's unique place of position and authority, which we rightly attribute to God's providence. Yet it was also her admission of her God-given ethnicity that saved her and her people.

The planned destruction came at the plotting of evil Haman, who had his heart set on a mass ethnic cleansing of the Jews. Haman, the resident Hitler of fifth century B.C. Persia, was an insecure man whose Agaite ancestors were ancient enemies of the Jews. Haman's pride fueled his anger against only one Jewish man, Mordecai, yet he was willing to use this as an excuse to commit genocide against a whole people group.

How often does the spirit of Haman surface in our own lives? Because of an offense committed against us by a single member of a family or perhaps of a particular ethnic group, we tend to condemn all people from that family or ethnic group. We need only to remember Haman's end—hanging on the gallows he had prepared for Mordecai—to realize this path of prejudice will only lead to our own demise.

A Jewish Man in the Culture of Greece

Unlike Moses and Esther, Paul (known before his conversion as Saul) grew up at ease in two different cultures. Paul was born in Tarsus, a port city greatly influenced by the culture of Greece. This Hellenistic influence sharpened many of Paul's scholarly abilities, which apparently included the study of Greek dialogue, poets and philosophers (see Acts 17:16–29). Paul's birth in Tarsus also afforded him his enviable Roman citizenship (see Acts 22:25–29). From all evidence in the Scriptures, Paul was no stranger to the predominant Greco-Roman culture of his day. Yet he was born a Jew, trained under the honored rabbi Gamaliel (see Acts 5:34; 22:3), and he later described himself as "a Hebrew of Hebrews":

> If anyone else thinks he has reasons to put confidence in the flesh, I have more: circumcised on the eighth day, of the people of Israel, of the tribe of Benjamin, a Hebrew of Hebrews; in regard to the law, a Pharisee; as for zeal, persecuting the church; as for legalistic righteousness, faultless.
> Philippians 3:4–6

Because Paul could live with ease with both Jews and Greeks, he was able to use both cultures to further the Kingdom of God. He could reason in the language and culture of the Greek philosophers of his day. He "stood up in the meeting of the Areopagus" (Acts 17:22) and addressed the men of Athens. And he could take a stand for Christ using his Jewish cultural background. At the synagogue at Iconium Paul and Barnabas "spoke so effectively that a great number of Jews and Gentiles believed" (Acts 14:1).

Roman citizen. Greek philosopher. Jewish rabbi. Paul was able to use his divergent cultures to further the purposes of his Lord and Savior Jesus Christ. Imagine how many churches would never have been planted if Paul had stayed within the confines of just one of his God-given cultures!

Reclaim Your God-Given Culture

Modern Christians tend to think of culture as something extra or even something "secular," when, in fact, no one can live outside of his or her culture. I am disturbed by the reports of Western missionaries who confuse their own cultures with Christianity. In years past, many European and American missionaries considered their own style of dress to be more "Christian" than that of other places around the world. As a result of these missionaries' teachings, many indigenous peoples today living in tropical climates feel as though they must wear white shirts with ties, or long dresses with gloves, in order to worship in church. Imagine how these folks must feel on the inside, constrained as they are to dress impractically for their hot and humid climates.

Such ethnocentric missionaries would have benefited from following the example set by the Jerusalem Council. I am more amazed each time I read the account in Acts concerning the Council's decision not to try to force the Gentile Christians into the mold of Jewish law. A dispute had grown into a heated debate about whether or not the Gentile converts should be circumcised according to the law of Moses. But the Council decided not to overburden the Gentile Christians with cultural nonessentials. James declared:

> "It is my judgment, therefore, that we should not make it difficult for the Gentiles who are turning to God. Instead we should write to them, telling them to abstain from food polluted by idols, from sexual immorality, from the meat of strangled animals and from blood."
>
> Acts 15:19–20

The most astonishing thing to me about the decision of the Jerusalem Council was how few demands it made on the Gentile converts. There were just those four practices at the end of the above passage that the Gentiles were told to avoid, each of which was directly associated with polytheistic religious beliefs and pagan temple practices. In their prudence the Jerusalem church was providing a strong reminder that the first commandment was the basis for true worship of God. The Jewish believers were proclaiming that there would be no other gods but the Creator God, and that anything hinting of a diversion from the first commandment would not be tolerated.

The early Church had the foresight to recognize that the Gentile converts might be tempted to fall again into polytheism if allowed any leniency in those four practices. The early believers also had the wisdom to recognize that God can express Himself and be worshiped through any culture, not just the Jewish culture, and that they should not restrict His sovereignty in dealing with non-Jewish cultural practices. This is a lesson in trusting God that many missionaries have forgotten over the years. It has resulted in churches more interested in controlling the lives of their converts than in teaching them to seek God within the context of their own cultures.

There are simple questions that should have been asked when missionaries looked at these issues of culture, such as: Does God prefer clothes that make people uncomfortable and will appear strange to others in the same culture? Does God really prefer the sound of an organ to that of a drum or rattle? Does God want to isolate new converts culturally from unsaved family and friends?

Such questions may appear trivial, but anything that diminishes God-given identity, undermines what is godly in our cultures and weakens the impact of the Gospel is, I believe, of fleshly or even demonic origin. Those of us from cultures that have been told that there is nothing good in non-Western or non-European traditions know how devastating such ethnocentric teaching is. It keeps people from coming to Christ because it asks them to believe a lie about themselves.

Think about Moses, who chose to relate to his Israelite culture even though he had not been raised in it, nor had he ever even *seen* the Promised Land of his ancestors Abraham, Isaac and Jacob. God moved powerfully through this man who reclaimed his God-given culture.

We are all born within certain cultural boundaries, but we have the opportunity, through exposure and choice, either to conceal or to celebrate elements of other cultures. My own experience is not unique.

I was born to parents from the American South. Their ancestry is a mix of Cherokee Indian, Irish, Scottish and English. Because the American South is a heavy mixture of these four cultures, I was influenced by them all. Yet as a child I made a decision to relate to the world primarily as a Cherokee Indian. While I have a "birthright" to all four backgrounds, I feel most contented in our Cherokee Indian culture. But this does not preclude my feelings about, let's say, the Irish culture. In fact, many elements within the Irish and Cherokee cultures overlap. Many of the Irish I have met call themselves "the Indians of Great Britain."

Because of America's unique history and immigrant composition, all citizens have a deeper heritage than just being Americans. Celebrating these other cultures gives Americans a broader platform, not a more limited one, on which to stand and relate to God and others. Nor did God make a mistake when He allowed this special blend of people to produce me. I declare with the psalmist: "Lord, you have assigned me my portion and my cup; you have made my lot secure. The boundary lines have fallen for me in pleasant places; surely I have a delightful inheritance" (Psalm 16:5–6).

Increasing Signs of Homogeneity

In spite of God's infinite wisdom, there is a great movement in America to use homogeneity (sameness) as a means for achieving success. Have you looked at the church growth section in a Christian bookstore lately? I mentioned in chapter 1 that the fastest way to build a megachurch, according to the experts, is to target a single ethnicity, race, culture or income. They do not come right out and say this, but an urge toward monoculturalism is easily identifiable in their prescriptions for success.

One pastor, following the plan as set forth in a nationally known bestseller in the area of church growth, told me that the group of people he was trying to reach was those with an annual income of more than one hundred thousand dollars. True to his intended purpose, his church is growing at an incredible rate and is full of wealthy white people. Although I credit the pastor and staff with genuine friendliness to all people, it is unfortunate that anyone from another race or with a lower income can spot these self-imposed standards on the very first visit to the church—which is also likely to be the last. And although we bask in the comfort of being around those very much like us (as we also discussed in chapter 1), diversity is a gift from God.

I once wrote a report for my denomination that proposed taking a dead or dying church in my city and pumping it up with a new name, new staff and some fairly drastic changes in philosophy and cosmetics. One of the leaders in the denomination heralded my proposal as the best he had ever seen and pledged to get it to several hundred pastors as a stellar example of what they were looking for in what they referred to as "church restarts."

Where my proposal differed from most others was that it was my intention to begin the first multicultural, multiracial church in that city. Out of more than fifty churches, none had anything more than a token of diverse cultural representation.

But the committee rejected my proposal. Afterward I phoned one of the officers of the committee to understand why it had been turned down. Their reasoning, it seemed, had to do with the lack of success they believed a multicultural church would have.

Again, take a good look at the following passage:

> There were staying in Jerusalem God-fearing Jews from every nation under heaven. When they heard this sound, a crowd came together in bewilderment, because each one heard them speaking in his own language. Utterly amazed, they asked: "Are not all these men who are speaking Galileans? Then how is it that each of us hears them in his own native language? Parthians, Medes and Elamites; residents of Mesopotamia, Judea and Cappadocia, Pontus and Asia, Phrygia and Pamphylia, Egypt and the parts of Libya near Cyrene; visitors from Rome (both Jews and converts to Judaism); Cretans and Arabs—we hear them declaring the wonders of God in our own tongues!" Amazed and perplexed, they asked one another, "What does this mean?"
>
> Acts 2:5–12

The people asked a good question: What does this mean? At least one answer to that question is that God intends a culturally diverse Church. It is apparent that, from Babel to Pentecost, He delights in His varied creation; and a diverse Church also reflects His delight.

Is it possible that what passes in America today as "successful church growth" is nothing more than a sophisticated form of racism and classism couched in religious verbiage?

Yes, God obviously intends for His Church to enjoy numerical growth. But if we have to violate the principles of inclusiveness and diversity, such as found within God's very nature, in order to achieve numerical growth, then perhaps our success is not a pattern to follow but an example to be avoided. Success without godly righteousness is not success at all. The end result never justifies the means.

Perhaps your own church is painstakingly monocultural. Ask the Father if the reason for this really reflects His heart, or if it is simply easier and more comfortable to reflect only one part of the Body of Christ. Comfortable, because one of the first responses to the challenges of a multicultural church is often fear.

It is true that there will be a high level of anxiety, along with new problems to work through. This comes as no surprise. But God has given us models in the Scriptures from which we can draw encouragement and support. Let's look at a few.

Romans and Galatians

CASE STUDIES
IN MULTICULTURAL CONFLICT

ALTHOUGH IT FEELS COMFORTABLE when two of us are alike—or at least when we *think* we are alike—the truth is, we are all very different. If you take a dozen people from the same race, ethnicity, culture, social status, political party or even age and put them in a shared experience, there will be a honeymoon period—but when the honeymoon is over, watch out! I have seen examples over many years, and so have you.

I have also observed what some have dubbed the "halo effect," that magic time that comes afterward and is achieved only with determination. After our initial disappointment that the others are so different from us comes the time when we work through our problems, get a sense that the other people are really not so bad after all, and make a commitment to remain friends.

Working through racial and cultural differences in the Church is not so different from working through the differences outlined above. Unfortunately, many of us leave our churches when the honeymoon is over, and we miss the joy of experiencing unity within diversity. The fact is, the more obvious the differences, the more honest we can be with each other from the start. How uncomfortable the dance we perform when we notice those obvious differences but try to avoid them in our conversations out of politeness or fear of offending the other person. Our fear is often based on the fact that we do not really know if we will reveal a prejudice in our own hearts—so we "dance."

I love unfeigned honesty! I realize there is a place for subtlety, but honest talk, especially in the area of multicultural relationships, is so refreshing! Native Americans like to joke about our differences rather than take them too seriously. One of our gifts is the ability to laugh at ourselves, so we tell a lot of jokes at our own expense. Our people have also noticed something over the years—that whites sometimes tend to take themselves too seriously. Perhaps one of the gifts we can share with the Euro-American Church is the ability to laugh at ourselves. Proverbs 17:22 says that laughter is good medicine.

It is with this in mind that I offer a story inviting the Native American to laugh at himself, the Euro-American to laugh at himself, and all the other people groups to laugh *at* us and *with* us.

How Good Do You Look?

They say a Texas rancher was looking to impress his neighbors with the quality of horse stock he could obtain. He had been told that an old Indian man in Wyoming raised the best horses money could buy, but the man was often reluctant to sell them to outsiders. The rancher set out for Wyoming, determined to come home with a prize. He arrived late in the day but was able to rouse the old Indian man away from his beans and fry bread, and together they went outside.

The Indian (we won't call him a rancher or cowboy so as not to confuse things—eyyyeee!) happened to have his best stock in the corral and began pointing them out to the Texas rancher. He made it clear to the rancher that he could have any horse in the corral for a fair price except a certain roan standing all by herself. She was not for sale.

"But she looks like the best horse you've got!" the rancher protested.

"No," replied the Indian. "That horse don't look so good."

The rancher, thinking the owner was just trying to drive the price up, began his best trading arguments. Each time the Indian replied, "That horse don't look so good." The Texas rancher, determined to have the roan regardless of the price, made the Indian man an offer he could not pass up. So the old Indian had his grandsons load the horse into the Texan's trailer.

The rancher was so excited that he phoned his friends and neighbors from his cell phone to meet him the next morning, and he drove all night to get home.

The next morning at the ranch, they began to unload the horse, but there was a problem. The roan began to run into things and stumble. Angry and embarrassed in front of his friends (whom he had already told how much he paid for the horse), the man loaded the animal back into the trailer and drove all the way back to Wyoming. He knocked at the door with determination. Finally the old man came to the door.

"You're a crook and a liar!" shouted the rancher. "I paid you good money for that horse, and now I find out you sold me a blind horse."

The old man, remaining calm, looked at the poor, worn-out Texan. In a quiet but sure voice he responded, "I told you once, I told you twice and I keep telling you over and again, but you don't listen. That horse don't *look* so good!"

Like the roan horse, when it comes to our many cultural differences, sometimes we don't look so good. As individual believers we need to look better at our brothers and sisters of different colors, and as local churches we need to look better in the eyes of the world, and reflect the multicultural heart of the Father. But that will not happen until we look deep within our own hearts to see what prejudice is still at home there. If we allow these prejudices to remain unchallenged, we miss an opportunity to be more like Christ, and for the Church to look more *like* Christ.

Most of us want to avoid the discomfort we face in interracial and multicultural situations. Here are two of the classic lines often heard in these uncomfortable moments: "I don't look at the color of a person's skin" and "I'm so glad God is colorblind." Let's get this straight: If you don't see my skin color, then you are not just colorblind; you are *totally* blind! And if God is colorblind, He sure did some good guesswork in His creation, especially with the rainbow!

Honestly, I know what people mean by these statements. What they are trying to say is, "God doesn't judge a person on the basis of race or culture, but rather on what's in his heart." The truth of this statement is commendable. But the stark reality is, our colors and cultures differ one from another. Statements like "I don't even see your skin color" lead some people to act as if they should be ashamed of their ethnicity, while our ethnicity is part of how God made us. It is a gift to be celebrated, not a handicap to be hidden.

If you want to truly reflect the Father's heart, then accept people as God made them, including their race, color, ethnicity and culture. Only at this point of acceptance can honest dialogue begin.

We should not fear ethnic or cultural conflict within the Church. In fact, the very first internal conflict in the Church—and the first opportunity for godly resolution—was a result of clashing cultures. The Greek-speaking widows felt that the Jewish widows were receiving preferential treatment in the daily food distribution.

> So the Twelve gathered all the disciples together and said, "It would not be right for us to neglect the ministry of the word of God in order to wait on tables. Brothers, choose seven men from among you who are known to be full of the Spirit and wisdom. We will turn this responsibility over to them and will give our attention to prayer and the ministry of the word." This proposal pleased the whole group. They chose Stephen, a man full of faith and of the Holy Spirit; also Philip, Procorus, Nicanor, Timon, Parmenas, and Nicolas from Antioch, a convert to Judaism.
>
> Acts 6:2–5

It is interesting to note that most of the deacons chosen to resolve this conflict—possibly all of them—had Greek names. In other words, the Church used great wisdom in choosing men from the culture that was being discriminated against, rather than Jewish leaders who might only give further cause for complaint. This deference to the minority culture was an honest attempt to preserve and protect Christ's witness among them—a lesson we would do well to remember.

Cultural Conflict in Rome

The apostle Paul addressed many cultural conflicts between Jewish and Gentile believers in his letter to the Romans. This may even have been one of his main reasons for writing this letter. It offers principles to us today as we consider how to work through ethnic or cultural conflict.

To understand the cultural discord in Rome concerning Jewish and Gentile Christians, we need to look at a bit of background. In A.D. 49 the emperor Claudius issued an edict expelling all Jews from Rome because of "continuous disturbances at the instigation of Crestus," which may be a reference to the teachings of Christ.[1] Considering the date of Paul's letter to the Romans, probably about A.D. 55–58,[2] it is very possible that the repercussions from this Jewish expulsion played a significant role in the relationship between Jews and Gentiles in Rome.

We can be fairly certain that the Roman church was not started by one of the original apostles. There is no mention in Scripture of its apostolic foundations, and we know Paul made it a point to preach where the Gospel was unknown, rather than "[build] on someone else's foundation" (Romans 15:20). It is more likely that the church at Rome began as a result of the events recorded at Pentecost, since "visitors from Rome (both Jews and converts to Judaism)" were recorded as being present that day (Acts 2:10–11).

There is no way of telling for sure, but if those visitors from Rome did begin the Roman church, they were likely either Gentile converts to Judaism or else Roman Jews. Either scenario would give the Roman church a unique beginning because of its Hellenistic influence. The many names mentioned in Romans 16 reveal a church made up of people from all walks of life, including Jews (for example, Mary in verse 6) and Gentiles (for example, the household of Narcissus in verse 11).

So when Claudius expelled the Jews from Rome, including the Jewish believers (see Acts 18:2), only Gentiles were left to lead the church. That means that for perhaps six to nine years, the church at Rome lost much of its Jewish influence.

There is no record of how long the edict of Claudius was enforced, but it is feasible to believe that by his death on October 13, A.D. 54, Jewish people were still not fully accepted in Rome. One can imagine how Jewish believers must have felt on their return to find their own culture—the culture that had given birth to Christianity—playing a diminished role in the everyday life of the church.

In light of these facts, Paul wrote to the church in Rome, where Gentiles likely now held most of the key leadership positions. There was at least some degree of animosity on both sides, and Paul went back and forth—addressing first Jew, then Gentile—continually throughout the book of Romans to describe the importance of both groups before God.

How Do Two Cultures Come Together?

Unlike the situation in Galatia, where Judaizers were forcing their particular Jewish cultural beliefs on the Gentiles, Rome provides the first record of a Christian church practicing a largely non-Jewish Christianity. I believe this is one reason Paul spent so much time in this letter teaching about the faith of Abraham. He wanted to be sure both Jew and Gentile understood that it is the circumcision of the heart, and not the flesh, that is important.

To keep things in perspective, we should remember that the believers at Rome also possessed many great attributes. Paul commended them because their faith had been "reported all over the world" (Romans 1:8). The overall picture we get is that of a flourishing church with readjustment problems as it tried to integrate two cultures into its daily life. In light of this conflict, Paul was able to give us a rich and wonderful historical and theological foundation for the Gospel.

It should also be noted and credited to the Roman church that there are no personal warnings within this letter such as we find throughout many of Paul's other writings. We see in Romans 2:1, and can infer throughout, that the apostle was speaking not so much to fleshly, carnal people as to those who had been influenced by a worldly philosophy with an exclusionist mentality.

The overall theme in light of the history and context of the book of Romans is this: *How do two separate cultures come together as one in the Christian faith?*

Facing Our Differences Together

In light of the cultural conflicts at Rome, the Holy Spirit, through Paul, gives us some tremendous principles for dealing with these problems.

Though himself a Jew, Paul began by stating his loyalties to both people groups, Greeks and non-Greeks, declaring himself "obligated" to both (1:14). Concerning their commonalities and differences, Paul defended the Jews because they were the first to receive the Gospel (1:16). But he went on to say that all people are justified only by faith (1:17). He further stated that Jew and Gentile are both under sin and cannot escape judgment except by salvation through faith alone (1:17–18). Paul hit the Gentiles hard (1:18–32), then turned it back on the Jews for their condemnation of the Gentiles (2:1–9). Next the apostle stated that the Jews' unique position will bring them, prior to the Gentiles, first judgment and then glory (2:9–10). Then Paul made the leveling statement that "God does not show favoritism" (2:11). He went on to defend the Gentiles who had lived by faith according to their own consciences (2:14–16), and then showed a broader picture of the law (2:17–29).

This alternating dialogue with the two cultures continues throughout the book of Romans. Rather than provide a commentary, I want to encourage us by mentioning some of the principles that aided the Roman church:

1. We should face our differences together, as our forerunners in the faith once did. Too often we choose sides and "divide the camp," when in reality we are all on the Lord's side.
2. We should encourage diversity in leadership. The apostle Paul's leadership and pastoral heart are evidenced by his courage to struggle with the multicultural issues of his day. The list of names in Romans 16 reveals great

diversity in gender, culture, ethnicity and economic status.

3. We should not shirk our responsibility because it may be uncomfortable, but search the Scriptures for answers as we seek to bring together various cultures in the faith. Too often we are motivated by worldly trends or by political correctness when, in fact, all our answers can be found in God's Word.

4. We should bring in peacemakers like Paul who have an understanding of the issues and can help us see from one another's perspectives.

Greater Conflict in Galatia

Paul showed even more daring in a situation when one group went too far in declaring its own culture as the "superior" Christian culture. When the believing Jews at Galatia begin to force their cultural beliefs on the Gentiles, we hear some of the harshest admonitions in the New Testament:

> I am astonished that you are so quickly deserting the one who called you by the grace of Christ and are turning to a different gospel—which is really no gospel at all. Evidently some people are throwing you into confusion and are trying to pervert the gospel of Christ.
>
> Galatians 1:6–7

And again:

> You foolish Galatians! Who has bewitched you? Before your very eyes Jesus Christ was clearly portrayed as crucified. I would like to learn just one thing from you: Did you receive the Spirit by observing the law, or by believing what you heard?
>
> Galatians 3:1–2

Foolish, a different Gospel, bewitched, even *perverted!* What is the perversion at Galatia? Two teachings of Jewish believers:

1. That the practices of Jewish culture, especially circumcision, justified them before God (3:2);

2. That Gentiles as well must observe Jewish culture (4:8–10).

The answer to this perversion is found in Galatians 5:1: "It is for freedom that Christ has set us free. Stand firm, then, and do not let yourselves be burdened again by a yoke of slavery."

Paul's argument in the book of Galatians for freedom in Christ applies to cultural divisions, too. The purpose of worshiping God in our own culture is so that we may be free in the *expression* of our devotion. How often I have seen Native American elders attending a worship service and been brought to tears as they expressed deep appreciation for seeing Jesus "finally worshiped in our own Indian ways."

In Paul's day the Judaizers—the Jews who wanted to bring the people under a system of cultural rules and religious bondage—threatened the freedom and very message of the Gospel of Christ. We have "Judaizers" in our day, too, metaphorically speaking, although they do not usually reflect the culture of Judaism, but rather of Euro-American cultural Christianity. According to Paul, however, anything that stands between my faith in Christ alone for justification is a perversion, because no human accomplishment can justify us before God—only Christ's work on the cross.

The modern-day Judaizers place too much importance on a cultural practice or the lack of some cultural practice. Any person can be considered suspect for any number of reasons, varying from how he or she wears his hair, to what method of baptism is used, to what day of the week he or she attends a church meeting. In Native American churches today, these legalists are most concerned that Indian people do away with their cultural forms of worship. The use of the drum, eagle feathers, smoke, sweat lodge and sometimes even singing in our own tribal languages are sure signs to them that we cannot be Christians, or at least not serious followers of Christ. Strangely enough, the culture they wish to force on their brothers and sisters is not even their own, but that of the Euro-American colonizers.

The experience Paul recounted of traveling with his friend Titus, an uncircumcised Gentile, is worth noting:

> Not even Titus, who was with me, was compelled to be circumcised, even though he was a Greek. This matter arose because some false brothers had infiltrated our ranks to spy on the freedom we have in Christ Jesus and to make us slaves. We did not give in to them for a moment, so that the truth of the gospel might remain with you.
>
> Galatians 2:3–5

Paul made a very bold statement by saying that, regarding the circumcision of his travel companion, the actual "truth of the gospel" was at stake. Quite a serious claim over what would seem a small cultural practice! As we know, it is not the practice itself that makes the difference, but when that practice (or the lack of it) is seen to have salvific or justification value. At that point it stands in sharp contrast with biblical Christianity.

Isn't it interesting, then, that when Paul was traveling with Timothy, also from a Gentile heritage, he did have Timothy circumcised (see Acts 16:1–3)? What was the difference?

Not compunction, certainly not legalism, but freedom in Christ! Elsewhere Paul wrote, "To the Jews I became like a Jew, to win the Jews" (1 Corinthians 9:20). During the mission that included Timothy, Paul encountered unbelieving Jews who would have become so distracted by Timothy's not being circumcised that they would not have been able to hear the Gospel. In the case of Titus, however, it was not unbelieving Jews, but rather believing Jews, who were pressing to have Titus circumcised. They should have known better than to try to add something to the Gospel besides faith in Christ.

This brings up an interesting point concerning our witness to those outside the faith. According to Scripture it is always the believer's responsibility to go to the nonbeliever. Nowhere does the New Testament exhort us to stand our ground and wait for those outside the faith to come to us and adapt to our culture. It is always our job as Christians to relate to the culture of the unbeliever:

> To the weak I became weak, to win the weak. I have become all things to all men so that by all possible means I might save some. I do all this for the sake of the gospel, that I may share in its blessings.
>
> 1 Corinthians 9:22–23

73

Today we have a plethora of churches expecting to reach the lost by creating a monoculturally comfortable environment for unsaved people to come to. Paul's prescription for reaching the lost, and Jesus' example, is much different. They call us to relate to the unsaved, in *their* cultures, at *their* comfort zones, not ours. Yes, it will be uncomfortable for us. We will have to leave our own cultures and experience new ways of doing things. But doesn't the fact that God calls us to this multicultural experience make it all worthwhile?

part 2

Opposition
to Diversity

6

How Big Is Your God?

JUST A FEW YEARS AGO some friends of mine, missionaries to Zaire of African descent, shared with me their surprise at the colonial attitude still found in many overseas missions today. They told me a story about their first months at the mission compound.

It seems that they were eager to begin learning the culture of the people, so it was not long before they invited one of the African workers in the compound to come to their home for dinner. The worker was so shocked, he did not know what to say. When my friends asked him what the matter was, thinking they may have offended him, he explained that theirs was the first invitation into a missionary's home in the many years he had been working for the mission! How very sad that in all those years, no white missionary had attempted to cross the cultural barrier and reach that common African worker.

To be sure, no first-time missionary has ever set out on his sacrificial journey by saying, "Pray for me. I'm getting ready to take the Gospel, wrapped in the ideas of colonialism from a Western European, post-Enlightenment, paternalistic approach, to a heathen people." Yet that is, in effect, the result.

In case you are wondering, we are going to pick on missionaries in the first part of this chapter, even though in the eyes of good Christian people this group is off limits for critique. It is necessary to review our history, in keeping with the biblical injunction "It is time for judgment to begin with the family of God" (1 Peter 4:17), so we do not repeat past mistakes. If more Western missionaries had treated aboriginal peoples all over the world without cultural bias, I have a feeling that more people in the world would know Christ today.

Don't get me wrong—being a missionary is a high calling from God. Sacrificing the personal comforts of home and putting your life and the lives of your family in peril is noble and courageous. What's more, the motives of many European missionaries in the past were generally pure. They sought to bring Christ to people all over the world. Unfortunately, pure motives do not guarantee the right approach or effectiveness.

Let me add to this disclaimer that I am speaking as an insider on the subject. I have been a commissioned missionary myself and have operated within the realm of the current paternalistic mission system. I also want to say that because most systems of government, whether church, state or business, operate on the principle of homeostasis (maintaining internal equilibrium), it is difficult to make positive changes even when needed. In other words missionaries, like everyone else, are people of their time and usually abide by the conventional wisdom. (In chapter 10, "Honorable Mention: The Good Guys," I seek to honor some of those rare missionaries who took the added risk to be God's prophetic voice among their contemporaries.)

In the meantime, horror stories abound of how missionaries have mistreated the very people they were trying to reach with the Gospel. These stories, some of them infamous, are told among indigenous peoples around the world. One of these is the enslavement of the California Indians in Spanish missions. Another is the destruction of family totems in the Northwest. The missionaries who chopped the totems down mistakenly thought they were idols rather than identifiable remembrances of special family members whose images were carved onto the totems, akin to family photo albums today.

The unfortunate presumption evident in the past missionary movement rests in two areas, which we will explore in this chapter. First, *most did not understand the depths of their own cultural bias;* and second, *they failed to realize that Christ was already at work among the peoples.*

May I share one of the less injurious stories that typify the cultural bias so often reported?

No Blankets, No Hair

During the 1890s, mission work among the Kiowa Indians of Oklahoma began to flourish. The Kiowa were courageous and skilled at war. Kiowas cherished their freedom and were responsible for many deaths among their enemies. They were, in the true sense of the word, a very proud people.

One particular Kiowa woman was converted to Christ and became, according to the missionary standard, refined. She attended Carlisle Indian School in Pennsylvania and was not eager to go back to the "blanket Indians" (meaning those who were still practicing the old ways, one of which was to wear a blanket as a wrap) in her native Oklahoma. Convinced by the missionaries there to come back to her people, however, and be an example for them, she returned. But before long this refined Christian Kiowa woman was married to a Kiowa man with whom the missionaries were not pleased. His ways were still largely those of "blanket Indians," and his marriage to the missionaries' prodigy was hard for them to take.

He was known for his long and lustrous black hair—which in the eyes of the missionaries provoked the situation all the more. They assumed that when a Kiowa man put his faith in Jesus, he would cut his hair short and discard it, along with much of the rest of his culture.

One woman missionary, who was particularly close to the Kiowa convert, pleaded with the man on a number of occasions to cut his hair. He would not. Finally she could take it no longer. She offered to buy the man's hair in order to remove the obvious evidence of this cultural embarrassment. He consented.[1]

If anything, stories like these demonstrating confused priorities should cause us to reexamine our own cultures and see if various practices are based on godly truth, as set forth in the Scripture, or if they merely reflect the worldly ideas of the day. We all wear cultural blinders and often fail to see how another

79

person's culture could possibly be as godly as our own. Consider this statement from a seventeenth-century missionary to the Mohawk Indians in what is now New York State:

> I am making a vocabulary of the [Mohawks'] language, and when I am among them I ask them how things are called; but as they are very stupid, I sometimes cannot make them understand what I want. Moreover when they tell me, one tells the word in the infinitive mood, another in the indicative; one in first, another in the second person; one in present, another in preterit. . . .
>
> Johannes Megapolenisis, 1642, Fort Orange[2]

Learning any new language can be frustrating, but this missionary's extreme cultural bias is evident and his condescending attitude unfortunately typical. He continued:

> When we deliver a sermon, sometimes ten or twelve of them, more or less will attend . . . and afterwards ask me what I am doing and what I want, that I stand there alone and make so many words, while none of the rest may speak. I tell them I am admonishing the Christians, that they must not steal, nor commit lewdness, nor get drunk, nor commit murder, and that they too ought not to do these things. . . . Then they say I do well to teach the Christians; but immediately add, "Why do so many Christians do these things?"[3]

The idea that one man should speak and no one else have an opportunity to contribute to the discussion must have been a cultural shock for the Mohawks. Most Native American cultures value a more democratic approach, such as set forth in the Scriptures in the concept of the priesthood of all believers. The other apparent shock to the Indians—that the religion the missionary preached seemed to lack the power to keep the Christians from partaking in those habits that violated their morals!—should shock us, too.

God Has Made It Plain

Sometimes our theological approach to missions is indeed startling, particularly in the eyes of those who believe that non-Western, "uncivilized" peoples are unaware of God in their lives before a missionary comes on the scene. Those with a narrower focus seem to believe that God has His eyes fixed solely on Europe, and that the rest of the peoples of the world are outside His purview.

According to the Bible, God did not wait to show up with the European missionaries. In fact, Paul states in the first chapter of Romans that both righteousness and judgment have been revealed to all people, and that everyone has a chance to know God:

> In the gospel a righteousness from God is revealed, a right-eousness that is by faith from first to last, just as it is writ-ten: "The righteous will live by faith." The wrath of God is being revealed from heaven against all the godlessness and wickedness of men who suppress the truth by their wicked-ness, since what may be known about God is plain to them, because God has made it plain to them. For since the creation of the world God's invisible qualities—his eternal power and divine nature—have been clearly seen, being understood from what has been made, so that men are without excuse.
>
> Romans 1:17–20

Theologians call this phenomenon *natural revelation*—we know about God first through nature; and it is indeed natural for the Creator, who is all-loving and all-knowing, to do every-thing within His power to bring the people He created into a more intimate relationship with Himself. He has been at work among all peoples because He does not want "anyone to per-ish, but everyone to come to repentance" (2 Peter 3:9).

I know firsthand the experience of natural revelation in the lives of one tribe with which I am connected. Years ago I was adopted, according to a traditional tribal practice, into a Kiowa Indian family. My Kiowa mother used to say, "We knew about God before the white man ever came. We knew He was all-powerful, all-knowing, sacred and holy. We knew He was dependable and worthy to be served. We even knew He was lov-ing. But we did not realize the extent of His love until we heard about Him sending His only Son, Jesus, to die for our sins." The Kiowa had a revelation of God and a value system based on that revelation.

81

According to the Scriptures, truth has been revealed to *all* people, and each culture over the years has been shaped according to that revelation. In fact, cultures are formed by a people group's observations and experiences, as well as their agreement or rejection of revealed truth. Listen again to Romans 1:20: "Since the creation of the world God's invisible qualities—his eternal power and divine nature—have been clearly seen, being understood from what has been made, so that men are without excuse."

Some cultures have, to a great degree, collectively hidden the truth—for example, the cultures found in the cities of Sodom and Gomorrah. Others, such as many Native American societies, honored and kept much of the Creator's revealed truth through their traditions. No culture is perfect, but in varying degrees God's truth has prevailed in most of them.

So where is God at work in the so-called pagan cultures? I will share a few stories (and there are many!) of God's presence among aboriginal peoples before the arrival of the missionaries. But first it is important for us to see that this idea can be supported by the Scriptures. Many examples can be offered of God working through men and women outside of the household of faith.

One of these—an ancient biblical example—is Melchizedek, the "king of peace" to whom Abraham paid a tithe (see Genesis 14:18–20; Hebrews 7:1–17). Melchizedek was called "great" (Hebrews 7:4) and is compared to Jesus, whom Scripture calls "a priest forever, in the order of Melchizedek" (Hebrews 5:6).

Abraham himself, as Paul notes in Romans 4, was accepted by God solely on the basis of his faith. Who was Abraham, after all, but an Iraqi who believed that the Creator God was the only One to be trusted and obeyed? Before Abraham there was neither Judaism nor Christianity; nevertheless many were in right relationship with the Creator, including Enoch (see Genesis 5:24; Hebrews 11:5), Noah (see Genesis 6:8; Hebrews 11:7) and Job (see Job 1:1).

Cyrus, king of Persia, was an "outsider" to Israel—that is, he lived after God's covenant with Abraham—yet God used him in a mighty way. It was Cyrus whose heart was moved by God to give orders for Judah to rebuild the Temple for the worship of Yahweh (see 2 Chronicles 36:22–23).

Sometimes God speaks His message through the most unlikely people, like Balaam's donkey and Balaam himself (see Numbers 22:11–12), as well as Saul's prophets (see 1 Samuel 19:20–21). For Israel's great King Josiah, not listening to the Lord's words through a pagan king was a fatal mistake. Neco, king of Egypt, had actually heard from God, and told Josiah, "Stop opposing God, who is with me, or he will destroy you" (2 Chronicles 35:21). But Josiah did not listen to the pagan king and was killed in battle.

The Truth Speaks

The Scriptures themselves speak clearly that the Creator of the universe cannot be held within our puny, preconceived ideas about Him. Sometimes we forget that God is not just the God of our group, church or religion, but the one true God over all peoples, groups and cultures. He is everyone's Creator and loves each person. He is always at work among all people, revealing the truth to them—which ultimately shows the way to Jesus Christ, who is Truth:

> "I am the way and the truth and the life. No one comes to the Father except through me. If you really knew me, you would know my Father as well. From now on, you do know him and have seen him."
>
> John 14:6–7

Jesus did not say that in Him we see a Man pointing to the truth found in the Father. Nor did He say that He was a reflection of the truth. No, His statement reveals that He is Truth itself, the walking embodiment of the Truth found in the Creator, God the Father—because Jesus *is* God! The implications of this statement are phenomenal. All God's truth is found in Jesus. If we want to see God's truth—and He is the author of Truth and cannot lie—we need only look at Jesus, and truth will be revealed.

The radical claim made by Jesus also gives us a standard by which we can measure everything else. Many questions can be answered as a result:

Question: Is God pleased with my life?

Answer: If I am doing what Jesus commanded—following Him.

Question: Is there any truth in other religions?

Answer: Only the things that point to, reflect or somehow represent Jesus.

Question: What things in my culture and traditions can be used to glorify God?

Answer: Only those things that point to, reflect or somehow represent Jesus.

Melchizedek, for example, was honored by the writer of Hebrews as a picture of Christ in another culture. But sometimes, because of our ethnocentric blinders, we do not recognize the truth even when it is staring us right in the face. Take, for example, the incident that occurred at Nazareth as recorded in Luke 4.

Jesus returned to His hometown synagogue and began to read Isaiah's prophecy of the Messiah. When He declared the fulfillment of the passage on that very day, the people continued to listen. After all, if God had sent one of their own to be the Messiah, or even if Jesus thought He was the Messiah, that was O.K. It was perhaps a lot to swallow—but that was not what caused His listeners to want to throw Jesus off the cliff. It was only after Jesus revealed the truth that God was at work outside Israel that they became enraged. In Jesus' words:

> "I assure you that there were many widows in Israel in Elijah's time, when the sky was shut for three and a half years and there was a severe famine throughout the land. Yet Elijah was not sent to any of them, but to a widow in Zarephath in the region of Sidon. And there were many in Israel with leprosy in the time of Elisha the prophet, yet not one of them was cleansed—only Naaman the Syrian."
>
> All the people in the synagogue were furious when they heard this.
>
> Luke 4:25–28

Just who did He think He was, anyway? Here was a teacher messing up their ethnocentric philosophy of religion, claiming that God has always been at work drawing people "outside the faith" to Himself. Jesus revealed their small faith by showing them how big God really is. Here was God's embodied Truth, pointing them to the way of Truth, and they could not receive it.

The people of Nazareth would not believe that God chose to send His prophet Elijah to a Sidonian widow instead of to a Jewish widow. They could not accept the fact that God healed Naaman the Syrian leper and left other Jewish lepers to their awful fate. They could not believe that the faith of "pagans" could surpass the faith of the chosen ones. And according to nearly all past missionary principles and endeavors, the Church does not believe it, either!

How Big Is God's Love?

I guess when it really comes down to it, it is difficult to accept that God loves those outside the Church as much as He does those inside. Perhaps it is even more difficult to admit that, when He so chooses, God can use those outside our established faith community as much as He can use *us*. But God truly is at work in the world, not just in the Church (which is what we would like to believe).

I had a wonderful grandmother whose name was Love (no kidding!). Anna Nettie Love had a special, rare gift. As a child I was a recipient of it, but I never understood it until I became an adult.

One day my sister Donna and I were joking about who Grandma Love's favorite grandchild was. Of course, we both thought we were. But as we continued to discuss Grandma's impartiality and generosity, we finally admitted that she made every one of the grandchildren (and there were many) feel as though he or she was her special grandchild—even the ones the rest of the family considered "outcasts." If my grandmother, a mere human being, could make us all feel like her favorites, imagine God's ability to enable all the people of earth to feel His special love for them!

God's love is great beyond all scope and measure. We just have no idea what a loving Creator we have available to us. We tend to focus on the cross as the ultimate expression of God's love for us, and so it is, but His love begins much earlier than that. There is a definite connection between "For God so loved the world" of John 3:16, and Genesis 1:31, which states, "God saw all that he had made, and it was very good." The reason God loves the world is that He *made* the world. His own image is on every human being, and God marks each person as a candidate for redemption.

The cross means much more when we realize it was Jesus Himself who made the earth. The writers of the New Testament understood the connection that we tend to miss. They wished to emphasize Jesus' unique role in the creation of the world. The Bible is clear that in the economy of the Trinity's function, the world was made *by* and *through* Jesus Christ. Consider the following Scriptures:

> In the beginning was the Word, and the Word was with God, and the Word was God. He was with God in the beginning. *Through him all things were made;* without him nothing was made that has been made.
> John 1:1–3 (emphasis added)

> He was in the world, and though *the world was made through him,* the world did not recognize him. He came to that which was his own, but his own did not receive him.
> John 1:10–11 (emphasis added)

> He is the image of the invisible God, the firstborn over all creation. *For by him all things were created:* things in heaven and on earth, visible and invisible, whether thrones or powers or rulers or authorities; all things were created by him and for him. He is before all things, and in him all things hold together.
> Colossians 1:15–17 (emphasis added)

> In the past God spoke to our forefathers through the prophets at many times and in various ways, but in these last days he has spoken to us by his Son, whom he appointed heir of all things, and *through whom he made the universe.*
> Hebrews 1:1–2 (emphasis added)

Many of us have gotten away from the Christocentric theology of the Scriptures. Often we mark Jesus' entry into history from His birth in the manger, but His love for all His creation was already apparent at the dawn of time.

Humanly speaking they say a mother's love for her child is the greatest bond of love on earth. Though it is hard to imagine anyone having a deeper love for my children than myself, and I watched all of them come into this world, I am in awe of a mother's sacrifice of love during childbirth. We hear stories of mothers making great sacrifices for their children, even acquiring supernatural strength in order to rescue an imperiled child. Jesus compared His own love of Jerusalem to that of a mother hen, spreading her wings over her baby chicks (see Matthew 23:37).

Because of His unique role as Creator, Jesus' love encompasses not only the children of Jerusalem but all His children all over the world. The second Person of the Trinity was willing to die for the whole world, because He had given birth to the whole world. God's love for us all is truly beyond compare!

The Marks of Jesus

Genesis states that each plant, bird, animal and human gives birth after "its own kind." It is rare to find a child who does not in some way resemble his parents. Nor is it difficult to look at the world around us to find God's mark. God's marks are often found in cultures as well. There are many elements, especially in monotheistic cultures, that bear God's truth. Since Jesus *is* Truth, the concepts in our cultures that are true must point, reflect or represent Jesus in some way.

The apostle Paul was able to find truth even in the polytheistic culture of the Greeks (see Acts 17:23, 28–29). Missiologists have coined a term for these occurrences. Don Richardson, former missionary among the Sawi tribe in Irian Jaya, calls them *"redemptive analogies*—looking for their fulfillment in Christ."[4] God has placed concepts, ideas, symbols or objects in every culture that will lead the people to recognize a particular truth in Jesus Christ. The Bible is full

87

of examples in Jewish culture, including the sacrificial Lamb (see Leviticus 14:13; John 1:29); the bread of the Presence (see Exodus 25:30; John 6:51); and the high priest (see Leviticus 16:32; Hebrews 2:17). The book of Hebrews alone is full of redemptive analogies.

Can you see, then, that it is a fallacy to think anyone could actually "bring" Jesus to any people? Long before anyone answers a missionary call, Jesus is already working His redemptive purposes among every people group in order to reveal Himself. The work of a missionary, therefore, is not to *bring* Jesus from one culture to another, but to *reveal* Jesus' already-present marks on that culture. And it is the privilege of every believer to assist God in pointing out that Jesus is the fulfillment of every truth in every culture.

My friend Dr. Suuqiina is an Inupiat man who has researched and written about an Inuit prophet named Maniilaq. Before his people's first contact with the white man, this prophet accurately predicted many of the coming technologies before the white man's arrival, including the telephone, the coming of fire-powered boats on water and in the air, and homes heated without fire. Maniilaq also had encounters with God, who told him He would send a great light to the earth in the form of the Word, or Christ.[5]

The Northwest Indian tribes tell stories of the birth and death of the Creator's Son and prophesying the coming of the Scriptures to those cultures.[6] Several tribes have stories relating a visit many years ago from one they believe to have been Jesus.

Many years ago the Cheyenne had a teacher named Sweet Medicine who lived among them, prior to contact with the white man, and proclaimed peace among the people. Among the Cheyenne there is a tradition of "peace chiefs" who help the people as examples in integrity and wisdom. They maintain harmony among the people and are truly leaders who serve. Sweet Medicine is said to have begun the peace chief tradition among the Cheyenne people, and his teachings are still highly regarded by traditional Cheyenne and taught by their peace chiefs today.

Compare the truth in Sweet Medicine's words, followed by Jesus' teaching in the Sermon on the Mount:

You chiefs are peacemakers. Though your son might be killed in front of your tepee, you should take a peace pipe and smoke. Then you would be called an honest chief. You chiefs own the land and the people. If your men, your soldier societies, should be scared and retreat, you are not to step back but take a stand to protect your land and your people. Get out and talk to the people. If strangers come, you are the ones to give presents to them and invitations. When you meet someone, or he comes to your tepee asking for anything, give it to him. Never refuse. Go outside your tepee and sing your chief's song, so all the people will know you have done something good.[7]

"Blessed are the peacemakers, for they will be called sons of God. Blessed are those who are persecuted because of righteousness, for theirs is the kingdom of heaven. . . . Do not resist an evil person. If someone strikes you on the right cheek, turn to him the other also. And if someone wants to sue you and take your tunic, let him have your cloak as well. If someone forces you to go one mile, go with him two miles. Give to the one who asks you, and do not turn away from the one who wants to borrow from you. You have heard that it was said, 'Love your neighbor and hate your enemy.' But I tell you: Love your enemies and pray for those who persecute you, that you may be sons of your Father in heaven."

Matthew 5:9–10, 39–44

Another Christlike leader among Native Americans was Deganiwidah. "The Peacemaker" (the name he came to be known by) first brought peace to the Mohawks by enlisting the help of a Mohawk chief named Hyohnwatha. On August 30, 1142, the Great Law of the five Iroquoian nations was ratified. This Law gave a voice to all the people and taught them to listen to even the weaker dissenters.[8] (Some scholars believe the Iroquoian governmental system was actually the model for the United States government.)

The Cherokee, my own tribe, tell a story that testifies to the concept of resurrection. It seems that a hunter became lost in the woods during a snowstorm. He found a cave that would provide him shelter, but as he backed into the cave, he felt what he knew to be a bear. As he started to run out, the bear spoke to him, convincing the man to stay for the rest of the winter and assuring him that he would be kept well-fed and warm.

Good to his word, the bear spent a good, safe winter together with the man in the cave. As spring approached, the bear told the man that his friends would soon come looking for him, that they would find the cave, and that when they saw the bear, they would kill him.

"No," the man objected. "I will never allow them to kill you."

But the bear calmed the man's fears, telling him that this all would happen as it should. He asked only that after they had dragged him outside and skinned and quartered him, the man cover the blood with a pile of leaves.

The man agreed to do this last favor for the bear.

Eventually spring came, and it happened just as the bear predicted. The men from the village found the bear and killed him. They dragged the bear's body outside, removed his skin and then quartered the meat. Then they started to lead the man in the cave back to the village. The man paused to cover the bear's blood with the leaves, as he had promised. As they started out on the trail, he looked back. There, to his surprise, was the bear rising up out of the leaves. The man watched him walk back into the cave. Neither said a word.

Do you realize there are *thousands* of stories with similar redemptive analogies throughout the world? To the Jews Christ would become the sacrificial Lamb. To the Cherokees He could easily have been known as *the risen Bear*. The Cheyenne and Iroquoian nations could have related to Jesus the Peacemaker if missionaries had taken the time and interest to know the cultures of the peoples. But the unfortunate result of mission efforts that fail to consider their own cultural bias is apparent among Native Americans today, which some estimate as having only a five percent churched population.

One final story of a redemptive analogy among Native Americans—that of the eagle feather. To Native peoples all over North America, the eagle symbolizes the belief that our prayers are carried to the Creator. The eagle is known among us as the bird that flies closest to the Creator, so his feathers are highly revered and used during times of prayer.[9]

Why would such a universal symbol exist among the Native peoples of America? Is it possible that God wanted us to understand the concept of an Intercessor praying to Him on our behalf, as in Romans 8:34, where Paul describes Jesus as the One who "is at the right hand of God and is also interceding for us"?

As a pastor I used to get asked by many Indians, when they called me to visit someone in the hospital, to please bring my eagle feathers. This gave me plenty of opportunity to introduce Romans 8:34 to them and witness to God's obvious love for our Indian people and share the idea that all eagle feathers point to Christ.

There are marks of Jesus in every culture. Perhaps God's people will soon begin to assist Him in teaching these marks and revealing them to the peoples of the world.

7

Race and Cultures Clash

OUR WAKE-UP CALL

I RECALL THE GUT-WRENCHING FEELING I had when the Rodney King incident sparked off rioting, looting and mass burning in Los Angeles—because I lived through the Detroit riots of 1967. I watched the fire-lit skies on many nights from my home 35 miles away. Never did I imagine that similar unrest would still be occurring thirty years later. Do people still burn American cities over racially incited occurrences? Yes, and Los Angeles will likely not be the last. What will prevent your own city from being next?

In this chapter we will consider trends that point to an actual increase in racism and ethnocentrism, and statistics that indicate a rise in multiculturalism, and we will reflect on how the Church should respond in the face of these trends.

One would think, after such atrocities as the Holocaust, Cambodia's killing fields, the policy of apartheid and the laws necessitating the U.S. civil rights movement, that man's inhumanity to man would have subsided by now. Unfortunately there are still many lessons to learn.

Certain names automatically conjure up mental images of racial or cultural wars. Just mention Northern Ireland, Palestine, South Africa or Kosovo, and most people can tell you about the clash of cultures occurring in those faraway places. But Americans have problems of their own at home, and problems are breaking out all around us that point to ongoing racial and cultural tensions.

Perhaps racism is not generally as obvious as it used to be. Most surveys show a decline in harsh racism. This might be because it is no longer politically correct to show bigoted attitudes; people's real feelings are often kept hidden. The National Opinion Research Center at the University of Chicago, in a subtle ongoing survey from 1972 to 2000, showed that many Americans today still hold to old racist stereotypes. The survey found that minority groups were perceived overwhelmingly more negatively than whites, and that African-Americans and Latinos were rated last or next to last in almost every characteristic measured.

Sometimes these attitudes are not so subtle. I was sitting in a restaurant one morning having breakfast when the conversation at a nearby table caught my ear. Three professional men sitting directly behind me were not trying to hide their discussion in any way. One was complaining about the local Indian tribe that had blocked a land purchase in which his company was involved. Then all three began to denigrate Indians in general. They moved on to another subject only after one of them said, "We used to be able to shoot them around here, you know."

There I sat.

I suppose that the lack of public displays of racism—this conversation notwithstanding—could seem like a positive indicator that racism is waning, but then again, hidden racist attitudes do not stay hidden forever.

A relatively new phenomenon has occurred in the last decade. The material cost of racism is now reported as part of the story. The cost of fire-torched or blown-up buildings, the expense of man-hours in law enforcement—such calculations seem to count more these days in the scheme of things.

For more than six months in 1990, there was a standoff near Oka, Quebec, between First Nations Mohawk, the Quebec Provincial Police and the Canadian Armed Forces. The problem began when the Oka town council planned to develop a golf course on sacred Mohawk grounds that included a meeting place and an old cemetery. The ensuing

93

standoff reportedly cost the Canadian government more than two million dollars. Perhaps thinking of racism in financial terms will finally reach a materialistic society such as ours.

Still, for most of us, the price in human life far outweighs financial considerations, especially when incidents cost us the lives of our children, as with the 1995 bombing of the Alfred P. Murrah Building in Oklahoma City. Only two years earlier, when foreign terrorists bombed the World Trade Center in New York City, Americans realized they were not immune to terrorism. But the young men involved in the Oklahoma City bombing represented a new kind of terror—the home-grown variety. They reflected the sentiments of the militia movement, neo-Nazis, skinheads, the Aryan Nations and other white supremacist groups that are flourishing right here on American soil.

One thing does not seem to change. Whenever there is an outbreak of racial tension in the news, it brings out old stereotypical attitudes in people. Just let a story hit about one racial group taking some radical action, and everyone you talk to has a comment about it. That is when words or phrases like *those people* and *us and them* begin to surface. Deep down we seem to have a definite line drawn by which we separate ourselves from those unlike us.

But no citizen of any country likes to think of his or her nation as having racial and cultural tensions. After all, the days of Indians being shot and black men being lynched for no reason are over. Aren't they?

Racism: On the Decline?

I was speaking at a conference in Richmond, Virginia, recently with Mohawk worship leader Jonathon Maracle. Jonathon shared a story about his minister father coming to Richmond many years earlier, when he saw a sight he would never forget. Near the city limits, the elder Reverend Maracle saw the remains of a black man hung from a tree, his body riddled with bullets. I am certain that image stayed with him his entire lifetime. How could one forget such horror?

Jonathon's story reminded me of a news event that had occurred only one year prior to our conversation. I am sure it was a great shock to many Americans to hear the fate of James Byrd Jr., the African-American in Jasper, Texas, who was chained by his ankles to a pickup truck by two white men on June 7, 1998, and dragged until he was decapitated. Many of us thought such horrors could not happen today—just as we got another wake-up call when a white man, Reginald Denny, was pulled from his truck in Los Angeles by assailants and kicked, brutalized and smashed in the head with a large cinder block soon after the Rodney King beating in 1992.

Unfortunately, if you are Native American in the United States, your people's oppression and the atrocities committed against them will probably not receive the national press attention that these stories got. On June 8, 1999, for example, the mangled bodies of Wilson Black Elk and Ronald Hard Heart were found lying next to each other in the tall grass near the town of White Clay, Nebraska. Do you remember the story? Not exactly front page news. But the two men were the latest in a long string of Native Americans who had been beaten to death just outside of the Pine Ridge Reservation in South Dakota, on the other side of the border from White Clay, Nebraska.

After no real investigation occurred, the American Indian Movement was asked to come in and help bring attention to the injustice. I had several friends involved in this protest, which included a prayer vigil. It amazed me that hardly anyone except those on the "Indian grapevine" knew of these protests or about the atrocities that had gone on in this community between Indians and whites for many years.

Incidents of racism are reported more and more on college campuses. ABC's *World News Tonight* reported on December 7, 2000, that there were between 2,000 and 2,500 hate websites on the Internet. The relatively new phrase *racial profiling* has been used to expose the targeting of minorities for police stops in large metropolitan areas and even by the U.S. Customs Service. Perhaps American racial and cultural offenses are not as frequent and widespread as the Chiapas and Rwandan massacres or Sudanese slavery, but they are as morally outrageous. They also suggest that the theory of assimilation, such as was promulgated in the Americanization movement in the first quarter of the twentieth century, will never work.

What Does the Future Hold?

Assimilation seems to be successful only if you have features that cause you to blend in, and not stick out, in the larger society—features such as are found in most people of Western European origin. Nor is the idea of America as a great melting pot based on a biblical worldview. According to the Scriptures (as we have seen earlier), every person is created and cherished by God. And if that person can be accepted by others, then he or she does not need to be assimilated by losing part of his or her identity.

Some argue, however, that loyalty to country does mean assimilation. There is a feeling among some that if a person becomes a naturalized citizen of a particular country, his or her only allegiance should now be to that country's culture. It would be difficult to identify a single culture in America, a land of immigrants (although some of the traits would have to include materialism, celebrity worship and a quick-fix mentality). But am I to think that, although God made me, He expects me to deny the ethnicity that constitutes my heritage?

Jesus' answer concerning taxes is applicable in this area, too: "Give to Caesar what is Caesar's and to God what is God's" (Mark 12:17). My ethnic heritage is not a gift to me from a particular government, but from the Lord. I can be loyal to my country, therefore, without losing my ethnicity or cultural identity in the process.

Then what does it mean to be the citizen of a particular country, and what role does the Church play? To answer the first question, we have to consider that the definition of citizenship in the New World has continued to change since the arrival of the first "boat people" in 1492. Where there is one dominant race or culture, it is easy for the members of that group to give a simple definition to the question, but as Bob Dylan once sang, "The times, they are a-changin'."

A September 1999 report titled "Minority Population Growth: 1995 to 2050," issued by the U.S. Department of Commerce, attempts to provide a glimpse of how America may soon look. Most people are aware that the minority population in the U.S. (meaning anyone except non-Hispanic whites) is on the rise, and they have likely noticed that their own workplaces, neighborhoods and grocery stores are becoming much more diverse. Here are some of the projections:[1]

- From 1995 to 2050 the minority population will account for nearly ninety percent of the total growth in U.S. population.
- Every minority group will represent an increasing share of the future U.S. population.
- People of Hispanic origin will become the most populous minority group by 2010.
- The minority population will more than double between 1995 and 2050, increasing by 169 percent, compared to just a seven percent increase for the non-minority population.
- From 2035 onward, the non-minority population will decrease in size.
- In 1995 the District of Columbia, Hawaii and New Mexico already had minority populations exceeding fifty percent of their total population. By 2000 California's minority population surpassed its non-minority population. And minorities in Texas will represent more than fifty percent of the total state population by 2015.
- Those four states plus the District of Columbia will represent one-fourth of the total U.S. population by 2015, and there will be thirteen more states that are one-third or more minority by 2025.
- The minority youth population will more than double from 1995 to 2050, while the non-minority youth population will decline.
- Every minority group will remain much younger than the non-Hispanic white population.

How Will We Respond?

As the population becomes more profoundly diverse, and the face of America changes, how will the Church respond? One of the grave dangers is our propensity to operate on the principle of pragmatism: If it works, keep doing it. This pragmatism has allowed Satan to lead us down a primrose path of comfort, while a great precipice awaits us at the end of the trail.

As neighborhoods become more integrated and diverse, the standards of homogeneity will not work. In fact, this Church model will have the opposite effect from the one it desires. As the population becomes more diversified, our temptation will be to reinforce the ghetto mentality of homogeneity rather than to embrace and celebrate diversity. In my reading, racial violence often occurs in neighborhoods that are "defended white." Monocultural churches that live by the philosophy of "like draws like" instead of healing the wounds of society, and regardless of what color "like" happens to be, will serve to deepen the wounds and create more mistrust.

As each ethnic group continues to gain exposure, we will experience more racial crises, yet have greater opportunities as well for cross-cultural friendships and marriages. These inevitable partnerships are, and will continue to be, a learning experience and celebration of God's great diversity among us. Wouldn't it be strange for people to have friendships and marriages and children that celebrate God's diversity, yet be unable to find churches where the very fabric of their being is not accepted? Where will those from such culturally diverse backgrounds go for godly counsel? What will it take for the monocultural Church of today to ready herself for the awaiting multicultural world?

Perhaps our unhealthy tendency toward homogeneity, which will be outdated in the near future, will finally be put to rest.

Once I heard a waitress ask a friend of mine, "What are you?" Immediately I knew what she meant.

My friend answered, "Biracial," which somehow has a more polite tone than *mixed blood, mongrel, breed, half-breed, mulatto, Creole, melungeon, mestizo, metis* or any other word that refers to a person of another race mixed with someone descended from white Western Europeans.

When we are confronted by the otherness of an individual or group, anxiety often rises. This is one reason it has been difficult for dominant cultures to accept mixed-blood people. Is your church and mine ready to accept biracial, multi-ethnic, multicultural people as gifts from God, or must we conform to the monocultural patterns presented by most American congregations? It is one thing to say, "We accept everyone regardless of who he is," and quite another to accept everyone and *appreciate* them. The former statement may attempt to squeeze everyone into an established pattern; the latter conveys the idea that "our church is more bounteous because of your presence."

Somebody said, "We're all gonna live in heaven together for eternity, so we may as well learn to get along now." How very true!—and how very sad that the one entity in our society founded by the Lord Jesus Christ has not been a safe haven for this learning, and for acceptance and most of all love. Jesus delights to see His Bride coming together in worship and witness, wrapped in peace and "living in color."

8

The Subtleties of Racism

AT THE OUTSET OF THIS CHAPTER I would like to offer two examples of how subtle racism can be.

First let me mention a friend of mine who is very proud of his Native American heritage, and he looks the part. But he is married to a non-Indian who does not support his Indian activities and culture. I have heard many people make the comment concerning this couple, "She doesn't like him to be Indian." Usually the reply comes back, "Then why did she marry an Indian?" Strange, isn't it?

The second example concerns the work I have done over many years for Christian colleges. One Indian college hired me specifically because of my experience, my perspective on what a Christian college should be and my Native American heritage. Because I know well the problems associated with this college, I was told at the beginning of our relationship to "hit the ground running."

The college had drifted a long way from its earlier vision as a Christian and Indian institution. Besides suffering from a high student attrition rate, low morale, unprofessional faculty and staff attitudes, underdeveloped technology and poor community relations, it also had some serious racial problems that were being ignored.

When another Native American administrator and I began to bring these issues up in the appropriate meetings, the discussions were met with strong resistance. One common reply to our concern: "But we have more than fifty percent Native American students." Strange how a system itself can become infested with racist attitudes, even if it is full of people from that ethnic group.

But strong minority representation, whether in a marriage, college, church or government, does not guarantee the absence of ethnocentrism. We usually think of racism in terms of isolated incidents in which the rights of a person or group have been infringed on, based on race or ethnicity. There are more subtle forms of ethnocentrism as well. I call the type of problem at the college for which I worked *systemic racism* or *systemic ethnocentrism*. In other words, although no one person in the system may have been displaying overt ethnocentric actions, over time the system itself has been corrupted, and it continues to perpetuate policies that negatively affect a particular minority group.

Systems of Ethnocentrism

Systemic ethnocentrism is perpetuated in governing policies (official or unofficial) that maintain an unhealthy ethnic or culturally biased status quo.

The official policy of most churches, for example, says that everyone is welcome. Many churches post these very words on their church signs. Yet unofficially a certain standard is set that speaks much louder to violators than the welcome sign out front. This standard may be in decor, dress, language or any other area within that church's culture. If you are visiting from outside the particular group (whether the difference is ethnic, social or financial), then you usually understand that you are welcome only if you can conform to the "comfort zone" of those who govern the system.

I heard a story about a large church in northern California that makes the point. The people in this church emphasized their Sunday dress. It was part of the culture of that largely homogeneous church to wear fine clothes to church on the Lord's day. One Sunday a family walked in that, as reflected by their clothing, was very poor. To their embarrassment,

the only seats available were right up front. As the usher
began to walk the family down the long aisle toward the front
of the church, an uncomfortable silence fell over the congregation, broken by whispered comments on the family's
shabby appearance. There were no welcoming smiles from
the church members still standing in the aisle, no extended
hands of friendship, only a sense of discomfort that people
dressed like this were making a public mockery of their
established church culture. The pastor, seated in the front,
did not say a word about the occurrence that day.

The next Sunday morning the pastor waited until the last
minute to come into the sanctuary. Upon his entrance, the
congregation was aghast. Here was their well-paid, highly professional minister dressed in a T-shirt and bib overalls! Had he
taken leave of his senses? Then, remembering the uncomfortable pause in the previous week's service, a few people
began to get the message. From the platform, as the service
began, the pastor commented that he would change his
clothes for Sunday morning services only when the people
changed their attitudes about those different from themselves.

It did not take long, as I understand it, for the change to occur.

Jesus set a different standard for His followers living within
the systems of the day. He was seen with the poor and the
wealthy alike, the fisherman and the tax gatherer, the priest
and the prostitute, the Gentile and the Jew. The early Church
was careful in all her policies to make sure no one was left out.
Strange how these systems of righteousness have now been
taken over by such worldly influences as to deem certain persons' ethnicity or cultures as less than our own. How do such
attitudes and policies originate? I have a few ideas, which we
will look at in this chapter. As the preacher said, it is "the little foxes that ruin the vineyards" (Song of Songs 2:15).

Because of our lack of exposure to people from other ethnic
groups and cultures, we can easily begin to view our own cultures or ethnicity as superior. We might make little comments,
or hear comments from others here and there, about a particular group. We might experience a bit of intolerance when we
witness an unpleasant display by someone from another culture. A little hard-heartedness here and a little condemnation
there—all these lead to the systems we now embrace, systems

that keep others out, that ultimately will allow people different from us to spend eternity in hell as long as we are comfortable. The irony of it all is that we claim Jesus is *in* these systems of ethnocentrism.

It is difficult to recognize error when it is so entrenched.

Once again, however, Scripture paves the way. When the apostle Peter, a devout Jew, decided to follow Jesus, his Jewish traditions stayed intact. After Jesus' ascension and the coming of the Holy Spirit, Peter separated himself from the Gentiles out of fear. It is no mistake that God chose him for the fateful vision of unclean food, subsequently confirming, through Peter's experience with Cornelius, God's own acceptance of the Gentiles. Peter should have known better.

And Paul made no bones about telling him so! I am thankful to read an argument in Scripture between two godly men. It helps me keep my feet on the ground when I see that these spiritual giants were, like me, human beings with faults. Here was Peter, an ethnic Jew, whom God humbled tremendously in order to send a message of acceptance to the Gentiles. Peter had to eat every word he had spoken in his ethnic arrogance against the Gentiles. What a sense of humor God has! But Paul was not laughing when he confronted Peter about his ethnocentricity:

> When Peter came to Antioch, I opposed him to his face, because he was clearly in the wrong. Before certain men came from James, he used to eat with the Gentiles. But when they arrived, he began to draw back and separate himself from the Gentiles because he was afraid of those who belonged to the circumcision group. The other Jews joined him in his hypocrisy, so that by their hypocrisy even Barnabas was led astray.
>
> Galatians 2:11–13

All ethnocentricity, racism and cultural discrimination is, as Paul says in the NIV, "clearly in the wrong." All systems that perpetuate these evils are, at the minimum, non-Christian in their approach. Our ethnocentric systems are so pervasive today that if you are on the inside, you will not even recognize them. But Satan does, and looks for ways he can invade these corrupted systems.

The human heart is capable of much good, but too often we allow sin to go unchecked. This seems especially true when it comes to ethnocentrism. Dominant cultures have always flaunted a notion of superiority, and find a "reasonable," sometimes "godly," rationale to support their claims and pardon their oppressive attitudes.

Although, if the truth be known, Western European–based people are probably no more ethnocentric than any other group. As human beings we are all prey to the same sins. But because Western European–based systems have dominated much of the world's recent history (witness the areas of philosophy, science, economics and theology), this ethnic group bears examination concerning how ethnocentrism develops in systems of oppression.

Let's look at the British as an example.

British Expansion: A Case Study

I have often wondered why the British have so often seen themselves as *the* "civilized" culture. Perhaps more than any other people, the British have tried to colonize the world and impress their ways on others. The British list of past and present "possessions" is immense and diverse, including colonies such as Belize, Bombay, Gibraltar, the Falkland Islands, Hong Kong, Jamaica, New Zealand, India, the Philippines, Canada and the Americas. In the movie depiction of the classic *The Last of the Mohicans,* the words of a young British officer express this idea: "I thought British policies make the world England." Indeed, if there were no competition, the whole world would *be* England!

Economics was the single primary factor fueling colonial expansion. Perhaps the drive to declare oneself superior to all other races and cultures is a rationalization that stems from greed. But whether ethnocentrism stems from that source or whether it feeds other sins is not our immediate concern. Either way, ethnocentrism is rooted in certain cultures and somehow transferred into a corporate psyche.

Generally, English gentry have thought of themselves and their culture as superior to most other cultures, but a quick glance into British history reveals a startling pattern and an example of how the subtleties of ethnocentrism develop.[1] Bear with me.

Settlement of the British Isles began thousands of years ago by an unknown people group, followed by men and women of the Bronze Age who came from the Western Mediterranean. Then came the Celts, who first appeared in history in Central Europe in the eighth century B.C. They colonized Britain in two waves, first from France and Germany, then from Roman Gaul (France). In 54 B.C. Julius Caesar invaded Britain and exacted tribute from the inhabitants. Rome left Britain alone until Claudius invaded in A.D. 43 and made it a province of the Roman Empire. The Britons lived under the rule of the Romans who settled there. Rome claimed the British Isles as its possession and condemned the Celts as savage barbarians.

During the Roman occupation (which lasted until A.D. 410, when Rome finally pulled its troops out), Scotland and Ireland remained unconquered, and their warriors—the Irish-Scots from Northern Ireland and the Picts from Scotland—continually launched attacks on Romano-Britain. In the same time period, Saxon pirates from North Germany, Denmark and North Holland also raided England.

After Rome pulled out, Britain was defenseless against the raiding Angles, Jutes and Saxons. By A.D. 530 most of England belonged to the Anglo-Saxons, who colonized the country. The native population, the Britons, put up considerable resistance to Anglo-Saxon expansion, but gradually, over a century and a half, they were either reduced to slavery or else they fled into the hills of the Celtic lands to the west and north.

Then came the Viking Age, commencing about A.D. 793 and ending with the defeat of the army of Harald Hardraada in 1066. The Vikings were Swedes, Danes and Norwegians—Scandinavians from a self-contained northern society that spoke a common language and shared a common culture. By 851 they had set up permanent camps, and by 878 had overrun all England except Wessex. The Saxons fought back, and until A.D. 1066 England was uneasily united, the Anglo-Saxons living in one part of Britain and the "Norsemen" (the

Vikings) in another. Sometimes the Anglo-Saxons ruled, sometimes the Vikings.

In A.D. 1066 the Normans—Vikings from Denmark who had settled on the north coast of France and intermarried with the indigenous Frankish-Gallo-Roman population—took over the rule of England, building castles to enforce their rule and making French the national (and mandatory) language. The Normans gradually assimilated into the local population, however, and by the time Henry II ascended England's throne in A.D. 1154, the Norman period had ended. In 1385 England went to war with France, and once again English became the patriotic language.

Why have I recounted this abbreviated history? Because of the evident pattern: British ethnicity and culture are inherently amalgamated, or mixed blood. It is possible that, hidden in the forced spread of British culture and its immediate disregard for other cultures, there is a deep *zeitgeist* of hidden shame that may originate from a corporate denial that Britons themselves are an extremely multicultural people. As the old adage goes, "Hurt people hurt people." Thousands of years of foreign cultural invasions and transitions would make it difficult for any people to be homogeneous, yet Britain has tried to force her presumed single culture on much of the rest of the world.

Perhaps British colonialism had nothing to do with cultural *pride,* but it is a result of a deep sense of cultural *shame.* This type of shame, which originates in the pit of hell, can have many damaging effects. Why are victims of abuse often likely to commit abuses against others? Because anger has to be let out somewhere. In the same way, perhaps ethnocentric cultures must claim superiority over others in order to nurture an aborted sense of self-worth. This is expressed in self-promotion or in displays of cultural superiority. To borrow a line from the great English playwright William Shakespeare: "The lady doth protest too much, methinks." In other words, if you are too vocal or forceful, you probably have something to hide.

Cultures that try to dominate others are always vocal about their own superiority. This may come out in an obsessive concentration on family lines and heirships. It may be revealed through the illogical value placed on pedigreed animals such as dogs or horses. Perhaps it even results in attempted genocide on people who are different. Britain's leading geneticist claims, ironically, that there is even more racial mixing in their gene pool than most Britons want to admit:

> One in five white Britons has a direct black ancestor, says the country's leading geneticist. Dr. Steve Jones, of the University College, London, used census figures to calculate that 11 million white British people have Afro-Caribbean blood relatives. His calculations will surprise many Britons who believe their families are from purely European stock. Dr. Jones said Afro-Caribbean people have been in Britain for so long they were now part of the gene pool. "Many people who think of themselves as white—although they may not want to admit it—have a black ancestor," he said. "We have to accept that the rivers of genes which flow through history run into each other all the time."[2]

Wouldn't God be more pleased if Britain embraced her diversity and pulled off the monocultural mask?

Mixed Bloods

The British and other Western Europeans have done an effective job expanding their culture over all the rest of the world and into every area of society, including Christianity. The earliest paintings of Christ reflect a man with physical characteristics of the Middle East. But as Christianity became more pervasive in Europe, the picture of Christ in the arts changed to reflect a more Western European image. Even today most movies about biblical characters must feature actors with English accents in order for us to "believe" them.

An African-American church leader once told me about an experiment he did in college. As part of his class report, he brought in a picture representing Christ as an African-American. He held up the picture and began to rip it slowly from top to bottom. No one in class said a word. Then he took a picture of the blue-eyed, light-skinned, sandy-haired Christ we are all familiar with and slowly raised it up. Knowing what he

107

was about to do, a group of students rushed at him and forced him to give them the picture. All the students were white.

But history tells of other expansionist cultures besides those in Western Europe. Discomfort with the "otherness of the other" is not limited to European nationalities. It can also be found among full-blooded Asians, Africans, Native Americans and in virtually every community on earth. Native Americans hunted one another and sold each other into slavery for their colonial mentors. Coastal African tribes also sold their inland brothers into slavery. Animosity between Asian groups, such as between the Japanese and the Koreans, is well documented. No human culture is exempt from the sin of ethnocentrism.

Racial superiority appears not only in cultures but in families as well. Think of the cruelty wrought against the progeny of people groups that harbor animosity toward one another. News reporters told us of the difficulties Amerasian children had, trying to survive in Vietnam after the war. Even today children of American couples—one black, the other white—face many obstacles.

There is a social game often played in the Native American community that targets mixed bloods. It tries to determine who is the "most Indian" or, as we say, the "biggest Indian." I call this the "Indian Urinating Contest." This game of one-upmanship is played by making statements concerning an individual's "credentials." One statement that usually wins this contest is "I'm a full blood [name your tribe here]." The implication is that if you are not a full blood, then you are less of a Native American. The U.S. government's "tribal blood quantum system" is set up to perpetuate this type of thinking.

Before the government set standards by which tribal members were to be recognized, most of our tribes never considered blood quantum as a standard for acceptance. But today nearly all tribes follow the government's deliberate plan for the eventual genocide of our people.

The same attitude exists in the minds of American citizens when they agree with this standard. But I believe this to be a form of worldly thinking and an affront to God. As Christians we have too often bought into this kind of thinking, which shows influences that are not only bigoted but demonic. If we equate the blending of physical characteristics from two races with a child's lack of worth as a human being, or at least with his or her inability to lay claim to a particular cultural identity, then we are, to say the least, being shortsighted. God has made each of us unique, with a unique heritage. The Creator has made no mistakes.

I have no doubt that God plans to bring healing in our day by lessening ethnocentric biases, and by saying to all, "Being Indian [or Anglo or Hispanic or Jewish or anything else] is not first a matter of blood quantum, or of what physical features are showing, but it is first a matter of the heart—of a God-given sense of belonging and of inherited ways of thinking and of sensing what life is about."

A wise enemy observes his opponent carefully. We have watched Satan spread his lies for thousands of years, feeding the social, political and religious justification for ethnic separation and cleansing. The time is long overdue for us to consider why it is so important for Satan to divide us along these lines. If vast destruction can be wrought by one lie retold in multitudinous ways, perhaps we should seriously consider the converse: *Can we stop listening to the lies long enough to hear God's truth of unity within diversity? How much glory will God receive by our simple telling (and living) of the truth in this area?*

9

Exposing
the Original Oppressor

SATAN IS NOT CREATIVE, so he just recirculates the same lies in every generation under new titles and different programs. He has only a few tools, but he uses them well. Wherever there is ungodly pride, disunity, disloyalty, usurped authority, division, greed or craftiness, we can be sure that demonic spirits are not far behind. It has been this way since the beginning:

> Put on the full armor of God so that you can take your stand against the devil's schemes. For our struggle is not against flesh and blood, but against the rulers, against the authorities, against the powers of this dark world and against the spiritual forces of evil in the heavenly realms.
>
> Ephesians 6:11–12

A spiritual battle is raging all around us. Unfortunately we often forget that human problems are fueled by demonic forces, and our forgetfulness breeds hatred toward our fellow human beings rather than toward Satan, where it belongs.

The particular demons that attack us, I believe, have specific duties and assignments. Two demonic characteristics I would like to examine in this chapter are *division* and *uniformity*. Because human beings fall easily for these deceptions, the enemy is able to play them century after century without much interruption.

Let's look at these two demonic spirits at work in a few movements of the last century that were indeed "crafty," and then discern Satan's goal for the Church.

What Comes Around Keeps Going

Charles Darwin's British cousin Francis Galton proposed the now-discredited scientific movement that later became known as *eugenics*. At the turn of the twentieth century the eugenics movement gave credence to the notion of a superior white race. Eugenics theory was about race improvement, and it focused on getting rid of hereditary disorders and flaws through selective breeding and social engineering. The foundation of eugenics was the drive to *divide* the races and *conform* everyone to a Caucasian model through genetic breeding and limiting non-Caucasian population expansion.

Eugenics theorists found fertile soil in America. Here was yet another pitch from the father of lies, just when the United States was ripe for such ethnocentrism. The Church, too, was susceptible to this theory. Charles Parham of Azusa Street fame was greatly influenced by eugenics theory as it was translated into theology. The sight of blacks, whites, Asians, Indians and Hispanics all loving each other in the joy of the Holy Spirit was too much for Parham to take. He sought to end what he perceived as doctrinal error by the "mixing of the races," and he succeeded.

On the other side of the country, the eugenics lie was being promoted in the civil arena. If Parham committed what amounted to spiritual murder in a street in Los Angeles by putting the kibosh on the formation of a multicultural church, Walter Ashby Plecker was committing documentary genocide in the commonwealth of Virginia.

Plecker ran the Virginia Bureau of Vital Statistics from 1912 to 1946. His main goal during those years was to expunge from the records any evidence of Native Americans living in Virginia. From Plecker's viewpoint there were only

111

two races, Caucasian and non-Caucasian, and Indians posed a distinct threat to the color line.

> After helping win passage in 1924 of an anti-miscegenation law called the Racial Integrity Act, Plecker engaged in a zealous campaign to prevent what he considered "destruction of the white or higher civilization."[1]

The twentieth century brought targeted mistreatment to Virginia's Native population, which was forced to take on the label *colored* (which at the time meant "African-American") on all legal documentation. Midwives who defiantly wrote *Indian* on birth certificates were fined or sentenced to jail terms. In 1943 Plecker issued a hit list of surnames of "mongrel" families that were not allowed to claim Indian or white ancestry. Most of these records have not been changed even today. Said Plecker, "Like rats when you are not watching [they] have been 'sneaking' in their birth certificates through their own midwives."[2]

Another result of Virginia's eugenics-influenced policies was the inability of the Indians in the state to receive federal recognition—a special status that allows Indian tribes to receive benefits from the federal government. The official state policy was that because there were no Indians in Virginia, they could not, therefore, be given federal recognition.

At the time of this writing, eight Virginia Indian tribes are still seeking recognition from the U.S. government: the Monacan, the Chickahominy, the Mattaponi, the Rappahannock, the Pamunkey, the Nansemond, the Eastern Chickahominy and the Upper Mattaponi. Official denial of their existence is ironic, since Virginia's Indians were some of the first to see the white men on the shores of North America, and since they signed the first treaties with England. (Remember Pocahontas, daughter of Powhatan?) The tribes still exist and would like to see Virginia's and America's racist policies reversed.

Unfortunately, eugenics scientific theory did not stop with documentary genocide. It was later embraced by Adolf Hitler and gave rise to his plans for a master race, which led to the eventual sterilization, torture and murder of millions of Jews, gypsies, Slavs and children of mixed racial heritage. To quote one source:

> [Eugenics was] rooted not in fringe, lunatic science, but in the mainstream of reputable genetics in what was indisputably the most advanced scientific and technological society of its day. The pursuit of genetic purity in the name of public health led directly to Dachau, Treblinka, Ravensbruck and Auschwitz. Steps to eliminate unfit or undesirable genes by prohibitions on sexual relations, restrictions on marriage, sterilization or killing are all forms of negative population eugenics (Kevles, 1995). Nazi judges and scientists ordered children killed or sterilized who had parents of different racial backgrounds or were thought to have genetic predispositions toward mental illness, alcoholism, retardation or other disabilities. This was done to remove the threat such children posed to the genetic stock of the nation and to avoid having to pay the costs associated with institutionalization and hospitalization.[3]

The only actual practice of "negative eugenics" in the United States that I have heard of (meaning the removal of "undesirables" from greater society) probably took place unofficially with vigilante groups such as the Ku Klux Klan, reputed to have castrated or murdered black men thought to have had intimate relationships (or even flirted) with white women. I mention another possible example in the Planned Parenthood discussion near the end of the chapter. Then there was the "Tuskegee Experiment":

> From 1932 to 1972, 399 poor black sharecroppers in Macon County, Alabama, were denied treatment for syphilis and deceived by physicians of the Unites States Public Health Service. As part of the Tuskegee Syphilis Study, designed to document the natural history of the disease, these men were told that they were being treated for "bad blood." In fact, government officials went to extreme lengths to insure that they received no therapy from any source. As reported by the *New York Times* on 26 July 1972, the Tuskegee Syphilis Study was revealed as "the longest non-therapeutic experiment on human beings in medical history."[4]

Although I have doubts about a direct connection between this notorious experiment and the modern eugenics movement, the study was conducted during the height of the movement, which created an open atmosphere for such atrocities to take place. It was no accident that those who suffered without regard were African-Americans, not whites.

Another side to this ethnocentric science, "positive eugenics," influenced Nazi Germany:

> On a smaller scale, the Nazis tried to encourage those who satisfied Nazi racial ideals to have more children. The most extreme form of encouraging eugenic mating was the Lebensborn program which gave money, medals, housing and other rewards to persuade "ideal" mothers and fathers to have large numbers of children in order to create a super-race of Aryan children.[5]

Although the theory of eugenics was only a scientific theory, it found its way into the Church in the form of social theology. We see milder forms of this philosophy in many areas of life today. Many of the church programs we have mentioned, ones that drift toward homogeneity as a goal, find their root in the religious spirits of division and uniformity. I have come to believe that religious spirits (demons that mask themselves in religion) carry the dual responsibilities of division and uniformity, for they work together.

What the Devil Really Wants

It is all about control. Division does not control; it merely disrupts God's control. Uniformity seeks to exert demonic control over people. What is Satan after? Illegitimate control over God's creation. Remember Isaiah 14:13–14, which addresses an evil king—and Satan himself— directly:

> You said in your heart, "I will ascend to heaven; I will raise my throne above the stars of God; I will sit enthroned on the mount of assembly, on the utmost heights of the sacred mountain. I will ascend above the tops of the clouds; I will make myself like the Most High."

Satan wants what he can never have—legitimate rule of the heavens and the earth. As we submit ourselves to the Creator, He gives us rule over His creation, and that makes Satan jealous. As we submit to one another in unity, diverse as we are, we have even more authority. Satan will go to great lengths to stop us from walking together in unity. He loves to use racial, ethnic and cultural differences (as well as many others) as reasons for disunity, and then conform us in an illegitimate uniformity, so he can achieve his goals of control through us.

Control in Churches

A clear example of this process occurred in a church where I once ministered. To many pastors, unfortunately, this story will have a familiar ring.

Two fighting factions were already present when my wife and I first came to the church. Edith and I were told by each group that we could not trust the other. The differences were really not about theology or carpet color; they were about control. The groups fought over such issues as who would chair the committees and who would decide the most minute details. It even went so far as jealousy when the leader of one group gave more money to the church than the leader of the other group.

Edith and I were resolved not to be dragged into such foolishness. Our goal was to restore control of the church to God. This meant we had to make some unpopular decisions, and as a result people got offended.

The group whose leader had given the most money was the first to leave. It took about six months for this to happen. In the eyes of the other group it was a clear victory (although none of this was spoken aloud—at least to our ears). But as time went on, the other faction grew more displeased with me and with some of the new Christians in the church. In the end, after about another year, the second faction left as well.

It was obvious to me that a spirit of division had been at work among these two groups before Edith and I had ever even heard of the church. Instead of conforming to Jesus Christ in unity (which would have been a miracle), we saw something of a "counterfeit miracle" take place. After both groups had left the church, they came together in a plot to have me ousted. Thirteen people from the two factions *conformed* with wholehearted agreement on a long list of complaints about me, then met with a denominational leader to have me removed.

If any of those complaints had been valid (they were not, in the mind of the denominational official), and if the groups had been following the leading of the Holy Spirit, this would have been a great show of unity in diversity. But instead of *diversity*, they yielded to *division*. In place of *unity*, they sought *uniformity*. To God's glory, however, and probably in spite of my efforts, five years later when we left that church, it was a great example of unity in diversity, including race, ethnicity and culture.

Becoming Like God

Whenever we work toward unity in Christ, a spirit of division will usually show up to try to rob God of His deserved glory. Church division can come through any circumstance, from the color of the people to the color of the carpet. In churches the job of the spirit of division is to get us thinking in terms of "us-and-them" rather than "Christ-in-us." The spirit of division polarizes and segments brothers and sisters in Christ.

Following close on its heels comes the demonic spirit of uniformity, whose task is to match people with similar sin attitudes. Division can work only temporarily; in order for Satan to have a lasting victory, uniformity has to take over. It is the task of uniformity to control—and that is at the root of Satan's plan. When the evil one can fire up ethnocentrism by influencing us to set up rules of acceptance or nonacceptance, he really does gain control over God's turf, at least temporarily.

The objective of control has been clear since the beginning. In the Garden of Eden Satan's goal was to divide Adam and Eve from their special relationship with their Creator. Adam and Eve were already in unity with God. They were "like God," made in His image. In the words of author Winkie Pratney, they were like God in a *godly* way. Satan's trick was to get them (and us) to try to be like God in an *ungodly* way. Remember his words: "For God knows that when you eat of it your eyes will be opened, and you will be like God, knowing good and evil" (Genesis 3:5). The desire to be like God in an ungodly way requires violating God's principles. Once we cross the threshold of disobedience, it becomes impossible actually to be like God.

When Satan appeared to Jesus during the temptation in the wilderness, his ploy was not to lead Jesus into ostentatious disobedience to God but rather to get Him to break God's commands by twisting what God had said. It does not matter if Satan is trying to divide a marriage, a friendship or a church. Once we cross the line of disobedience to God's commands, we have sided with Satan. Once we allow division in our ranks on any ungodly basis, including on the basis of race or ethnicity, we cannot be in true unity. Once we allow division, we are forced to seek uniformity.

Have We Helped God Out?

Uniformity is easily spotted. I remember my hippie phase in high school. I wanted to be seen as a radical nonconformist so, ironically, I wore clothes and chanted slogans like millions of other youths. We all wanted to be different, so we all acted the same. Are our churches any different? Many congregations want to be Spirit-led and independent, so they act like all the other churches around them. It is refreshing—but rare!—to walk into a church that is unique in and of itself because God has led it to be that way. I have been in hundreds of services in many states, in all types of denominations, and have found few that are truly unique.

Surely the Creator of the universe has more imagination than to lead a church into intentional and willful homogeneity! Is it God who demands that our churches meet at the same times every week? Is it the Holy Spirit who leads people to worship according to a routine order of service, then dismisses them within a prescribed time frame? I could go on. . . . If God is absent from our churches—and in many ways He is—I believe it is because we have simply bored Him away!

117

We would never give Picasso (or Dorothy Sullivan) a paintbrush and only one color of paint, and expect a masterpiece. We would not give Beethoven a single piano key and say, "Play us a concerto." Yet we limit our Creator in just these ways, seemingly expecting so little from Him that He can do much less than He wants within most of our churches. Few of us have had the faith to believe for our churches the way Jesus believes for His Church. No wonder Satan can steal, kill and destroy us! We believe his homogeneous lies as God's anointed truth. Not only have we grown comfortable with the lie, but we have actually learned to propagate it on his behalf.

Satan's presence is manifested through his works. He strives to thwart God from receiving His deserved glory. In the end we know that Satan loses, but whenever human beings cooperate with him, in the past or in the present, God's glory is often postponed and the kingdom of darkness prevails for that time over the Kingdom of light.

Demonic Connections

Consider a time in American history when Satan used these tools of division and uniformity in a tragedy that occurred about a hundred years before the eugenics movement. The division-uniformity lie—that instead of *diversity* we yield to *division,* and in place of *unity* we seek *uniformity*—caused the forced removal of the Cherokee Indians from our homelands.

For generations our lands, stretching in a long arc across eight Southeastern states from Alabama to Virginia, had been stolen from us through fraudulent or broken treaties. In the fall of 1838, after Appalachian gold was discovered in our territory, Cherokee peoples were rounded up and forced into stockades, where many died of disease and exposure. The people in the stockades were given little or no medical care and forced to eat raw corn and rotten pork. Dysentery was common and paved the way for other diseases. This existence degraded a people who had enjoyed freedom and great dignity. After almost a year of imprisonment, the Cherokees were force-marched to Oklahoma on a long winter trek in what was called the "Trail of Tears." One out of every four died on the march from cold, hunger or disease.

I have heard that the three main Cherokee prison camps were the model used by the military during the Civil War, where countless thousands of Union and Confederate soldiers suffered and died at places like Andersonville, Georgia. Prussian military advisors during the Civil War took the same ideas back to Europe, where they eventually influenced the associates of Adolf Hitler. Coincidence? I don't think so. Quite a coup for Satan in just about a hundred years! Remember that his tricks just get craftier over time; they do not go away.

Where was the Church during these atrocities against the Indians? To be sure, there was public outcry against the treatment of the Cherokees by individual missionaries, as well as others, but all the denominations involved in mission work to the Cherokees condoned their removal. (The Baptists later reversed their decision, at the urging of their missionary Evan Jones, and condemned the removal.) God's "official" Church, in other words, abdicated her mandate for righteousness, thereby contributing to the greater atrocities that would be committed later.

Our first reaction is usually to say that the Church had nothing to do with this or that injustice—for example, the genocide of World War II—but I wonder how God, who is not bound by time and geography, views it?

Perhaps there are certain trends in today's biomedical programs and research that smack of eugenics theory. Is it a coincidence that Planned Parenthood's turn-of-the-century founder, Margaret Sanger, was a member of both the American Eugenics Society and the British Eugenics Society?[6] Or that "the abortion ratio for blacks is about two times higher than that for white women," according to the Centers for Disease Control, and that the rate of abortion for Asian-Pacific islanders, Native Americans, Alaska natives and those who list their race as "other" is 1.3 times higher than that of white women?[7] Again, I don't think so.

Here is Sanger's perspective decades ago:

> Those least fit to carry on the race are increasing most rapidly. . . . Funds that should be used to raise the standard of our

civilization are diverted to the maintenance of those who should never have been born.[8]

Satan makes connections between movements and personalities, even if those connections escape many of us. The evil one does not care if people's lives are extinguished through philosophy or war or even "compassion" for single parents, just as long as he can kill those who might bring honor to the heavenly Father. Consider the genocide of surgical abortion. Forty million have occurred since the Supreme Court's infamous *Roe v. Wade* decision of 1973,[9] and each of those lives was meant to bring honor to God.

There are, no doubt, other demonic connections, if we are shrewd enough to pick up on them. Perhaps your own church has bought into the lie of uniformity. (I hope not!) A number of churches are now beginning to see the value of unity in diversity, although we have a long way to go. I believe that God, who wants such churches even more than you or I do, will exponentially bless the efforts of any congregation that abandons division and uniformity and travels down the path of unity within diversity.

part 3

Restoration Through Diversity

10

Honorable Mention

THE GOOD GUYS

A GOOD WAY TO DEFEND ONESELF against a lie is to speak the truth. Even better is to *live* the truth in the midst of the lie. Jesus Christ is God's living response to the lies of Satan. In the short period of His life, death and resurrection, Jesus dealt the death blow to every lie that had ever been told and that would ever be retold.

I have recounted a few sad stories in previous chapters concerning the indigenous peoples of the world and the distorted way Jesus has been presented to them. Rightly have I given these accounts, for when we expose the lies of the past, they will be more difficult for Satan to reuse. Most indigenous peoples testify to horrific wrongs that have been done them by colonialism; and regrettably they also share the sad news that most Western Europeans do not really want to hear about what their ancestors did to the host peoples of the land. It is often difficult, therefore, for First Nations peoples to hear or even believe that there were other colonizers or missionaries who treated the host peoples with honor and dignity— people who, like Jesus, lived the truth. But as followers of Jesus we need to hear truth.

In the past several years there has been much criticism over a "revisionist" approach to history. Because history is often

123

"the lies of the victor," as Napoleon said, it is often one-sided. But to compensate by exposing only the negative aspects of history, or by trying to distort historical truths to fit our own worldview, is another worldly way of reacting. God's Word calls us, rather, to "[speak] the truth in love" (Ephesians 4:15). That means we must share not only the bad news but the good news as well. And one aspect of truth-telling is to honor those who have faced the consequences of being people ahead of their time.

There were honorable men and women who spoke and lived the truth amid the lies of their time—men and women of distinguished valor when it came to rejecting the conventional wisdom of the day that supported those twin demons we looked at in the last chapter, division and uniformity.

Every community has its heroes in this regard. The great missionary Hudson Taylor is said to have dressed in common Chinese clothes and worn his hair in a queue. Bruce Olson, an American transplanted in the Colombia/ Venezuela jungle, is virtually a Motilone. In this chapter I would like to cite some examples of people with this kind of courage and commitment who related in years gone by to the indigenous peoples of North America.

Please understand that these unsung heroes may also at times have acted in ways that did not benefit the indigenous peoples. They were not perfect, or even at times consistent, but at some point they stood with Jesus over and against the standard paternalistic missionary practices of their day. Perhaps we can learn a few lessons from those who have gone before us, and find inspiration to be people ahead of our own time.

Thomas Mayhew and the Praying Indians

Although the earliest colonists in the New World have attracted much criticism for their treatment of the host peoples, some among them displayed a sincere love for the Indians and, by all recorded accounts, treated them fairly. The goodwill of Thomas Mayhew Sr. and his family toward the Wampanoags is praised by a number of historical writers.

Mayhew purchased the islands of Martha's Vineyard and Nantucket as well as the Elizabeth Islands in 1642. His family settled off the coast of Massachusetts and organized a church the following year. In that same year Mayhew's son, Thomas Mayhew Jr., began evangelizing the Indians with the assistance of Hiacoomes, the first Indian to be ordained as a Protestant in America. By 1674 there were fourteen towns of "praying Indians."[1] I have recently met a group of Christian Wapanoags whose ancestors were among those first converts.

The Lenape and William Penn's Holy Experiment

According to seventeenth-century British law, any resistance by the native inhabitants of land claimed by England marked those inhabitants as enemies of the Crown. So when William Penn received a charter to Pennsylvania from King Charles II, it was seen as preposterous for the English Quaker to assert that the Native peoples living on the land he had bought should be petitioned and dealt with in a fair manner. Fortunately Penn's convictions held longer than his time of being ridiculed.

Penn was able to found Pennsylvania as a "Holy Experiment" in 1681 with the full blessing of the Lenape (Delaware) people. His approach was one of friendship, fairness and peace that was established without weapons. He joined the Indians in their struggles and in their celebrations. Penn was known to have danced wildly with his Lenape friends in at least one celebration. Penn genuinely loved his Native neighbors and they loved him as well. "I have made it my business to understand [their language]," he wrote, "that I might not want an Interpreter on any occasion. And I must say, that I know not a language spoken in Europe that hath words of more sweetness in Accent and Emphasis, than theirs."[2]

William Penn's words reflect the heart of a man who loved not only his Indian brothers but God as well. Here is part of an address to Chief Tammany, a Lenape chief of great influence, in June 1683:

> The Great Spirit, who made me and you, who rules the heavens and the earth, and who knows the innermost thoughts of

men, knows that I and my friends have a hearty desire to live in peace and friendship with you, and to serve you to the utmost of our power. It is not our custom to use hostile weapons against our fellow-creatures, for which reason we have come unarmed. Our object is not to do injury, and thus provoke the Great Spirit, but to do good.

We are met on the broad pathway of good faith and good will, so that no advantage is to be taken on either side, but all to be openness, brotherhood, and love. I will not . . . compare the friendship between us to a chain, for the rain may rust it, or a tree may fall and break it; but I will consider you as the same flesh and blood with the Christians, and the same as if one man's body were to be divided into two parts.[3]

The Lenape, in respect and admiration for Penn, made him a chief among their people. Chief Tammany said of him, "We will live in love with William Penn and his children as long as the creeks and rivers run, and while the sun and moon and stars endure."[4]

Sir William Johnson, Friend to the Mohawks

William Johnson was not a missionary but a businessman whose fair treatment of the Indians made him a powerful figure during the French and Indian War. Johnson came to America from Ireland with his uncle in the mid-eighteenth century, and almost immediately made inroads for trade with the Mohawks in what is now New York State. His honesty, coupled with his adaptation to Mohawk life and culture (to the point where he dressed and spoke like a Mohawk), earned him the respect of the Iroquois Confederacy and eventually the position of *sachem* (chief) among the Mohawks. After the death of his first wife, Johnson took Molly Brant, sister of his close Mohawk friend and apprentice Chief Joseph Brant, to be his wife.

An effective military leader, Johnson was allotted vast land holdings in the Mohawk Valley, as well as a knighthood. On one of his trips back to England, Johnson also became a follower of Christ. Although he secured permission for several missionary endeavors among the Six Nations (the Iroquois Confederacy after it was joined by the Tuscarora in 1722), it is reported that he often took issue with the missionaries and their methods. Land speculators in addition to missionaries held Sir William in contempt for his efforts to preserve Indian lands and halt expansion.

Sir William Johnson was often called on by the Indians and whites for his influence as a peacemaker. Mohawk Chief Abraham recommended that Johnson be made their agent. In 1755 Johnson received an appointment as Superintendent of Indian Affairs, with full powers to deal with the Six Nations in the British interest. He served in that influential position, often upholding the rights of the Indians, for many years. Sir William is given credit for negotiating the Treaty of Fort Stanwix in 1768. He continued as a businessman until his death in 1774.[5]

Evan Jones and the Cherokee

When Evan Jones answered a call to assist the missionaries to the Cherokees, the recent émigré from Wales probably had little idea what the work would entail. But in 1820 he and his large family set out on their long journey from Pennsylvania to the Valley Towns area of North Carolina. In a short time, due to the attrition of former mission staff, and to Jones' surprise, he became the missionary in charge.

The Valley Towns mission, in the heart of the Middle Settlements among the full-blood Cherokees, was almost always in need of basic provisions, and Jones often got into trouble with the Baptist denominational accountants and administrators. He was also criticized by jealous co-workers and became the target of occasional violence from local white vigilante groups. Nevertheless he set a standard that, in my opinion, has yet to be equaled by American missionaries among Native Americans.

The main tactic of the colonies in their prior wars against the Cherokee had been to wage war just before harvest time and force their deaths through starvation and disease during the cold winter months. Also, as the whites encroached on the land, traditional Cherokee hunting grounds, as well as farming and gathering places, became fewer and less productive. The Indians, in turn, became more dependent on government and mission donations just in order to survive.

It was stated by a denominational administrator, in criticism of Jones, that he "feeds and clothes every poor and wandering Indian who crosses his door." His white neighbors in North Carolina and, later, Oklahoma resented his treatment of Indians as equals and abhorred his strong abolitionist views. Yet he was a close friend and confidant to Chief John Ross and the Cherokee Council. Jones was the only non-Cherokee appointed by Ross to assist in leading one of the detachments on the Trail of Tears.

Evan Jones, and later his son John, worked closely with Cherokee minister Jesse Bushyhead, one of the most respected men in Cherokee history. Jones labored to learn the difficult Cherokee language. At first he was very critical of traditional Cherokee beliefs, but later he modified his views. In Oklahoma, under Jones' influence, the exercise of traditional Cherokee religion, such as the stomp dance, was even allowed to take place on church grounds.

The Joneses' work among the Cherokee, along with that of the Reverend Jesse Bushyhead, resulted in dozens of trained Cherokee pastors, many of whom later became Cherokee national leaders; more than seventy churches and "preaching stations" in the old and new (Oklahoma) Cherokee Nation; and thousands of conversions to Jesus Christ. Other results of the Jones's efforts include the translation and compilation of a Cherokee New Testament; a Native Bible training school where everything was spoken, read and written in the Cherokee language; the revival of many godly Cherokee religious beliefs and principles (which other missionaries had tried to expunge); a Cherokee printing press and newspaper *(The Cherokee Messenger)*; and many so-called "mercy ministries."

Evan and John Jones were both made full members of the Cherokee Nation in their lifetimes.[6]

Bishop Whipple and the Dakota Sioux

The Right Reverend Henry B. Whipple was made the Episcopal bishop of Minnesota in 1859. No other church leader, it is said, had as much influence on behalf of the Indians at that time. Bishop Whipple was a great advocate for them. He used his position of authority to write letters and articles for magazines and newspapers, to speak to government officials (including the President), and to conduct public speaking tours in Eastern cities to make the needs of the Indians known.

At the end of what was called "Little Crow's War" in 1862, hundreds of Dakota Sioux surrendered to the U.S. Army, thinking they would be considered prisoners of war. Instead they were tried as war criminals. Many of the trials lasted less than a minute and consisted of just one person, sometimes even a child, stating that a particular warrior had participated in a raid. The government was determined to hang those Indians. This great injustice would eventually occur at Mankato, Minnesota, in the town square and would become the largest mass execution in the history of the United States.

Ample testimony was presented during the trials that many of these warriors had not been involved in any raids whatsoever, but the testimonies were not given due weight. In the end, however, Bishop Whipple was able to use his influence to persuade President Lincoln to commute the death sentences in favor of lighter sentences for 269 of 307 men.[7]

Isabel Crawford and Saddle Mountain

Isabel Crawford's name is probably familiar primarily to the Kiowa and Comanche people of western Oklahoma. She was trained as a missionary in Chicago and set up her tent near Saddle Mountain, Indian Territory, in 1893. The Kiowas were among the last of the tribes to be placed on a reservation.

Right from the start Miss Crawford did things differently. As a single woman coming to serve a patriarchal culture, she faced many obstacles. But against a system of missionary paternalism, which had already been well established at the other mission churches, Isabel Crawford would make her mark—indeed, God's mark—with the Indian people in the Saddle Mountain area.

When told by a Kiowa warrior that he could never follow the Jesus road because it would cause him to be less of a Kiowa, she responded, "Following Jesus will make you more of a Kiowa, not less." And she meant it, because for the most part

129

she did not impose the rigid standards of American culture with the same vigor as her missionary compatriots.

As is the case with many innovators, Miss Crawford's success was also her downfall. Saddle Mountain was reportedly the only mission church in that area that was raising up Native lay leaders and deacons who could actually run the church without the help of the missionary. In protest, on one of her trips away, the other missionaries stirred up enough trouble to have her removed.

Isabel Crawford's time among those people was not long in years, but she is still remembered fondly by hundreds of Kiowa and Comanche elders as the woman who was brave enough to share Jesus—or "Jeesah," as they say—a Jeesah for their own people.[8]

More Good Guys

The list continues with people like Count Nicolaus Ludwig von Zinzendorf, famous for founding the Herrnhut Christian community in Europe in the eighteenth century. He told the Moravian missionaries sent to the New World not to expect the Indians to live like the people in Europe.

James B. Finley, Methodist missionary to the Wyandotts in Ohio from 1821–1827, was an extraordinary champion of Indian rights and served as a negotiator to protect Indian lands during a time when most people thought there should be no Indian rights at all.

Abolitionist John Beeson was a reformer who, after fighting to end slavery, turned his attention to improving the situation of Native Americans in the nineteenth century. Beeson kept the plight of Native Americans before the American public, including securing a promise by President Lincoln to work for justice on behalf of the Indians at the close of the Civil War.

This list is not meant to be comprehensive but rather representative of those who have lived the truth among America's indigenous peoples. I imagine there are stories from every continent and island in the world representing the same principles in different contexts.

The Bible says, "Give everyone what you owe him: If you owe taxes, pay taxes; if revenue, then revenue; if respect, then respect; if honor, then honor" (Romans 13:7). As indigenous peoples we are called to honor those who have been honorable on our behalf. Were it not for these brave people and others like them, who risked not just their social standings but their careers, sometimes even their lives and the lives of their families, we might have no true witness of Jesus in our Native communities.

11

Finding Identity in Our Cultures and Nations

THERE IS A MYTH IN CHRISTIANITY that has to do with our identity. This myth has engendered poor theology and, as a result, a misunderstanding of the very nature of humanity. Here is how the myth goes: Because human beings are fallen, corrupted by sin, we are therefore worthless, without value.

Human beings are helpless when it comes to saving ourselves, but we are not worthless. After God made human beings (as well as everything else in creation), He "saw all that he had made, and it was very good" (Genesis 1:31). God blessed the man and woman and gave them the responsibility to be keepers of the earth (see Genesis 1:28). When Adam and Eve disobeyed God, they broke relationship with Him. Were they still made in God's image after the Fall? Yes. Would their children be made in God's image as well, even though they were born into sin? Again, yes.

To be made in God's image means at least that we are of great value to Him. If we were not, then He would have discarded us. The fact that He continues to try to relate to us and allows us to relate to Him, despite our grievous sin, shows us that we have value. Jesus, God's decisive expression of relationship with us, the final sacrifice for sin on our behalf, is the ultimate substantiation of our value in God's eyes.

Every time I see Dana Carvey and Mike Myers do their "we're-not-worthy" routine, I am reminded just where our worth comes from. It has nothing to do with our own accomplishments, and everything to do with the One who made us.

Antiques Roadshow is one of my favorite television programs. People bring in old junk from their attics and they bring in items that end up being worth thousands of dollars—but I cannot tell the difference. I have learned that whether something is a piece of junk or a great work of art depends on one of two factors—the skill of the artisan and the rarity of the piece—and often only the expert can assess this. Only pieces from the most skilled masters of their medium bring in the big bucks; and the rarer a piece is, the more it is worth. If it is an original and there are no others like it in the world, it might be quite valuable, even priceless.

Our value as human beings is founded on the same two criteria. We were created by the greatest Artist of all time; and every human being is an original, with no "copies" possible. By these standards we have extreme worth. In our case, too, the Creator is also the Expert who makes the determination, and we have to take His word for it! We have value because He made us to have value, and because He says that we do.

People sometimes use the fact that we are stained by sin to justify their own "worthlessness." But since God is the One "who wants all men to be saved and to come to a knowledge of the truth" (1 Timothy 2:4), those who are sin-stained (that's all of us) and even the unredeemed are still worth something to God. The price Jesus paid to redeem us was enormous, and like a good investor, God wants to have His prize in His own possession.

In Philippians 3:8, after a discussion of his Hebrew identity, Paul said he counted "everything a loss compared to the surpassing greatness of knowing Christ Jesus my Lord." In fact, "I consider [all things] rubbish, that I may gain Christ." That was not to disown his ethnicity, and it was certainly not to denigrate his worth to God; it was to devalue everything in light of Christ's incomparable worth. Paul of all people was keenly aware of his Jewishness. In Romans 11:1 he asked, "Did God reject his people? By no means! I am an Israelite myself, a descendant of Abraham, from the tribe of Benjamin." He spoke longingly of the salvation of "my own people" (verse 14), and in the previous chapter he exclaimed, "Brothers, my heart's desire and prayer to God for the Israelites is that they may be saved" (10:1).

So the issue of biblical identity is an important one. As followers of Christ we know that our identity comes from God alone. Psalm 100:3 tells us: "Know that the LORD is God. It is he who made us, and we are his; we are his people, the sheep of his pasture." Just *how* did the Lord make us? (I do not mean mechanically but artistically.) Acts 17:26 states, "From one man he made every nation of men, that they should inhabit the whole earth; and he determined the times set for them and the exact places where they should live."

Have you ever heard anyone talk about himself or about someone else as "an accident"? This Scripture is telling us that we are *not* accidents. God has determined exactly *where* each of us will live and precisely *when* each of us will live there. This means God was able to look down the great genealogy chart of life, starting with Adam and Eve, and determine when, where and to whom you and I and "every nation of men" would be born. Our ancestors' ethnicity was not hidden from Him, nor was their culture. He knew it all. The phrase *he made every nation of men* uses the Greek word *ethnos* for *nations.* In other words, God made our ethnicity.

Think about your own heritage. It is not by accident that it may include several ethnic backgrounds. Ephesians 2:10 says that "we are God's workmanship, created in Christ Jesus to do good works, which God prepared in advance for us to do." God placed you in your family line for His purposes, and He planned it all before the foundation of the world (see Ephesians 1:4–6). Wouldn't it be a great blessing if you could recognize that much of who you are is God's choice, not yours? You had no choice about who your parents would be, or how you would belong to them, or where and when you would be born, or what your native language would be, or any of the surrounding circumstances. The particulars of your existence were God's selection, and His choices are always the best.

Everything God makes has value, and He continues to make good stuff!

Are Cultures Worth Something?

Did God plan our cultures as well?

As we discussed in chapter 6, God has allowed Himself to be known through His creation. When this happens, we sometimes make "markers" for ourselves concerning this revelation. God often instructed people to make memorials, for example, in order to remember something He had done for them. (Joshua 4:7 is just one example.) When we take a material object and give it spiritual meaning, then that object becomes a symbol. Part and parcel of every culture are symbols and how they are used.

Ceremonies are also part of the makeup of a culture. A ceremony is a special time and way of doing something, for a specific purpose. At certain events Americans observe the raising of the Stars and Stripes. The flag symbolizes the United States of America, and it carries other meanings as well, including liberty, the union of the fifty states, and patriots who have fought and died for our country.

Traditions are also part of culture. These can simply be observances that are repeated—for example (staying with the flag analogy), the Pledge of Allegiance to the flag. At my children's elementary school they perform this ceremony every day. The fact that it is repeated makes it a tradition or, some might say, a custom. Other customs can include the food we eat, songs we sing, stories we tell, our language and our dress style, just to name a few areas.

Customs can actually reveal truth. Since all truth is God's truth, it shows up in many different cultures in many different ways. When that truth is revealed to a human being, something must be done with it. One option is to hide it, but the Scripture is clear that when people "suppress the truth by their wickedness" (Romans 1:18), or "reject the truth and follow evil" (Romans 2:8), or "[exchange] the truth of God for a lie" (Romans 1:25), there are terrible consequences. A culture not based on truth is based on lies.

Rather than hide the truth of God's "natural revelation," we can accept and embrace it. To embrace the truth means to do something in order to reveal (rather than hide) it. This is why people make up songs and stories based on God's truth as revealed in their cultures. They create ceremonies based, again, on God's revelation of truth. They even paint pictures based on divine revelation. Any number of actions can be performed to develop a culture that is based, to one degree or another, on truth.

No culture is perfect. Every culture has a mixture of both truth and lies at its foundation. Cultures that have developed many of their ceremonies and customs on revelatory truth come much closer to being godly than those that have built their ceremonies and customs on suppressing the truth.

Just as our worth is determined by God, so He has given us godly elements in our cultures to identify with as well. Our cultures, then, are part of our identities. I may have been born in a culture that has honored God. For me to ignore those elements in my culture that are based on God's truth is foolish. I want to know not only where God has spoken in my culture, but where He has revealed truth in other cultures as well. Conversely I want to know what in my culture is based on a lie, so I will not be influenced in a negative way by it. This is all a part of the process of finding one's identity.

How Do We Identify Ourselves?

The Scriptures give us at least three valid ways that we can identify ourselves culturally—through birth, marriage and adoption.

The Birth Heritage

Americans tend to think of birth heritage as the only valid means of identity. Birth as a means of ethnic heritage and biological identity is affirmed numerous times in the Bible. How many times is the phrase *the son of* used in Scripture to show a biological connection? Too many for me to count! One need only note the number of times different genealogies are listed in Scripture to see the importance God places on our biological birth lineage as part of our identity.

Often when a foreigner joined the ranks of Israel, his or her ethnicity was pointed out, such as in the case of "Shammah son of Agee the Hararite" (2 Samuel 23:11). Because we do not know much else about Shammah except that he was one of King David's mighty men and that he was one tough dude, we cannot say why God had the writer mention the fact that Shammah's father was a Hararite. Perhaps it was to explain some of his cultural differences. Maybe he was acclimated to Israelite culture, but God did not want Israel to forget that some of the toughest guys in the army were not Israelites. I don't know. I only know it is there, and that if it is there, it is important to God.

The Marriage Heritage

The Bible also lists marriage as a means of identification. Scripture affirms the amalgamation of identities in marriage by declaring that the two "will become one flesh" (Genesis 2:24). If bride and groom are from different cultures, then a wonderful diversity is created.

My wife and I are from two distinct cultures. Edith was reared on an Indian reservation; I was brought up in country, city and suburbs at various points in my life. Our families are from different regions of the country. Her tribal influence is Shoshone; mine, Cherokee. Edith and I also have differing ideas about how certain things should be done, especially during the holidays. I get the most excitement out of celebrating Thanksgiving; she gets more enthusiastic about Christmas. And the list goes on. One of the things that has made our marriage rich is learning to appreciate the things that are meaningful to the other. We have grown close enough to learn to appreciate events and celebrations through the eyes of the other, and we are both richer for it.

Two becoming one also means we need to drop the things about our cultures that are ungodly. Ruth, a Moabitess, married Boaz, a Hebrew, and became not only a Jew but a progenitor of Jesus. Although Ruth came from a people whose culture was enveloped in idolatry, she made a decision to follow the ways of the God of the Israelites. Does this mean she was no longer a Moabitess? I don't think so. She is called that five times in the book of Ruth, up to the day Boaz married her and the book ends. No, I think she was a Moabitess who had embraced the truth of Judaism and shed all vestiges of her old culture that were based on idolatry.

Let me note that God's warnings in the Old Testament about Israelites marrying people from other nations had nothing to do with their race or culture, but rather with the likelihood of idolatry as a result. Ruth had declared, "Your God [will be] my God" (Ruth 1:16). Even Jesus' bloodline was mixed at several points with the very nations with whom God had forbidden intermarriage.

Marriage is not about losing our culture and identity; it is about integrating the identity and culture of the other person with our own identity and culture. The image of Christ as the Bridegroom and His Church as the Bride is a beautiful picture of our new identity with Him in marriage. We do not lose our culture and identity; rather, we begin to see life through His eyes.

The Adoption Heritage

The third means of God-given identity in the Scriptures is that of adoption. One beautiful example includes Ruth and Naomi. Naomi accepted her daughter-in-law as her own. Ruth's words that we summarized in the last section—"Your people will be my people and your God my God" (Ruth 1:16)—are redolent with God's good intentions for identity through adoption. Another covenant adoption in Scripture is that of Jonathan and David (see 1 Samuel 20:17).

Many Native tribes still have adoption ceremonies and practices that reflect these biblical principles. My tribal adoption into a Kiowa family was not in the least bit trivial for them, or for me. Without their invaluable help I would have been culturally lost when I lived among them. At the same time, because of my adoption, I was able to comfort my adoptive mother as a son during her final years of sickness. I was adopted as a son to another Kiowa family as well, and as a nephew to a Comanche/Kiowa couple. I was also accepted as a brother to a Cheyenne man, and as a nephew to a Cheyenne woman. Because of these special relationships, I will always have a deep and heartfelt affinity with these families and tribes.

Adoption of outsiders is a practice among my tribe, too. The custom of adopting persons from other tribes was in place long before the white man appeared in America. The Cherokee adoption process is undertaken most often to replace a lost relative, but not for that reason alone. An adopted person is taken into the same clan as the Cherokee who adopts him or her. All rights and responsibilities of the clan are then expected of the person who is adopted. The fact that he or she is white is insignificant to the Cherokee once the person has become a clan member.

Adoption is one way to extend families and create loyalties that will last beyond our own lifetimes. I once asked my Kiowa mother about some of her ancestors who were mentioned in the book I was reading. I said, "Which of these Kiowas are my relatives?" She replied with great sincerity, "Every Kiowa is your relative!"

One time, as I was undergoing a season of slander, my Kiowa father stood to his feet in a church meeting and said, "Libby adopted Randy as our son. I expect everyone to treat him with the same respect that you would my other sons." After that, much of the attack dissipated, because all realized that adoption is an important tribal tradition and not to be regarded lightly.

The Scriptures convey the same sense of sincerity concerning adoption. This act is a strong form of covenant-making, and God takes covenants very seriously.

Consider the treaty, or covenant, that Israel made with the Gibeonites under Joshua's leadership (see Joshua 9). In this example a whole tribe was adopted by another tribe. Although deceit was used on the part of the Gibeonites, in order to avoid annihilation, Israel knew that God expected her to keep the covenant regardless. Hundreds of years later, King David inquired of the Lord as to why there was a famine in the land. God replied that it was because Saul had broken Israel's covenant with the Gibeonites. God took the covenant so seriously that He punished Israel hundreds of years later for violating it (see 2 Samuel 21:1–9). Adoption is a very strong covenant.

Sometimes I run into people who have absolutely no idea what their bloodlines are, due to special circumstances such as childhood adoption. One phrase I often hear is, "I have no identity—I'm adopted." But from God's perspective this is not a correct way of looking at ourselves. In fact, an adopted person has two rich sources of identity—his or her birth identity and his or her adopted identity. Although the birth identity may be hidden from view (at least for a time), the adopted identity is just as valid.

The Heritage of My Nation

Birth, marriage and adoption are all ways we find our biological, ethnic and cultural identities. We also have a national identity through our birth country. Because I live in America, I have a distinct cultural identity that is recognizable anywhere in the world. Whether I am Native American, Irish-American or German-American, I will likely be recognized by others around the world as American. Although the country is a blend of cultures, being American is a cultural identity in and of itself.

I have enjoyed meeting Australian Aboriginals, New Zealand Maori and other indigenous peoples from all over the world. As indigenous peoples we have many things in common. But during those times with indigenous people from various parts of the world, I realize how much I have in common with the people of America of whatever cultural background. Regardless of my ethnicity, I will always be an American.

And so it is with every one of us, born in America or in any other country. We all carry many identities within our identities, and these can be used for God's purposes, whether we are Native, white, black, Asian, European, African, Polynesian or something else. As human beings each of us has a deep well of identity from which to draw. From God's perspective there is no such thing as "just plain vanilla"!

Our Lord Jesus Christ is God's premier example of identification. Jesus was born to the tribe of Judah, at a particular time in history, in a special country, to a specific family. Through Jesus' birth He intimately identified with all human beings and demonstrated once again the value of all His creation. Through Christ's death on the cross, He identified with the actual and potential evil of all human beings for all time.

"God made him who had no sin to be sin for us" (2 Corinthians 5:21). And through His resurrection Jesus restored hope to all people.

God chooses to identify with us at our capable best and in our contemptible worst. He is a God who relates to all His children in every culture. Can we say we belong to Him and do any less?

12

Head and Shoulders, Knees and Toes

IT IS GOD WHO GIVES NATIONS their true identities, just as He does individuals. But the United States has not yet realized her God-given identity, and I am afraid we have substituted an American myth for God's intended purpose.

I mentioned in chapter 7 that the great melting pot myth was never God's plan. Those who are assimilated or "melted into the pot" are generally left feeling culture-less. A melting pot is like a stew. All the flavors blend together to make a new taste, and each original taste is subsumed in the larger stew and thus lost. Someone has used a better analogy for America—a "tossed salad," meaning that the many different flavors and colors toss around in the bowl and complement each other, while none is lost. Perhaps God plans that we become either stew or salad, as need warrants.

But the United States has a long history of trying to restrict other peoples' cultural identities in favor of a false American identity. We have seen evidence of the full-scale effort over several centuries to obliterate the Native American culture—an attempt that did not work. We continue to expect other cultures to "melt" as well. As many nations continue to pour into America, perhaps we should figure out why. Could God Himself be allowing our land to become a land of many nations for a reason? Remember from the book of Revelation that we retain our ethnicity even in heaven:

> After this I looked and there before me was a great multitude that no one could count, from every nation, tribe, people and language, standing before the throne and in front of the Lamb.
>
> Revelation 7:9

Since God has a purpose for our ethnicity into eternity, we may as well use it here on earth!

God has given us many tools to carve out our identities, in order to help us view ourselves rightly and to relate to others. From God's perspective I am not just Randy Woodley, an isolated individual, but I was born within a particular family, into the Bird clan, into a tribal group called Cherokee, in a certain region of the United States, and with other ethnic DNA from Scotland, Ireland and England—other families, clans and tribes.

Ponder your own heritage for a while.

Because I live in North America, I can easily relate to other North Americans, especially those from the U.S.A. But I can also relate to many indigenous cultures around the world. (Incidentally, everyone's ancestry is indigenous to somewhere.) Because I am a male of the human species, I can particularly identify with other males on the planet. And as a representative of *Homo sapiens*, I should be able to relate on some level to any other human being.

In many ways I have as broad an identity as I will allow myself to accept. It is the broadness of our individual identities, as well as their specifics, that God uses to accomplish His purposes.

In our experiences of moving in and out of these sets of broad and narrow identities and relationships, we can find appreciation of unity within diversity. The relaxation of being around others like us gives us a sense of belonging. Anxious anticipation of being around those who are different from us pricks our curiosity and should lead us to explore and invest ourselves in the world outside of ourselves.

National Treasures

I have always enjoyed the splendor of diversity among languages and geography and culture. We need only open our front doors to view the magnificent extravagance of variety that God has bestowed on His creation in the flowers, insects, birds and creatures of the animal kingdom. Most of us enjoy these differences daily, but sometimes we fail to appreciate the same beauty and extravagance of variety that He has bestowed on people. The Creator has gone to great lengths to make us all unique.

His great desire is that in our uniqueness, we all reflect the love of Jesus Christ. The cementing factor of unity is love. From love flows appreciation for the uniqueness and similarities of others, as well as acceptance of the factors we cannot yet appreciate. It is love that binds our hearts together—regardless of and because of our differences—and enables us to learn how to live together.

It is always refreshing to look at one of God's definitions of love and see how those words apply to intercultural relationships:

> Love is patient, love is kind. It does not envy, it does not boast, it is not proud. It is not rude, it is not self-seeking, it is not easily angered, it keeps no record of wrongs. Love does not delight in evil but rejoices with the truth. It always protects, always trusts, always hopes, always perseveres.
>
> 1 Corinthians 13:4–7

Sin, by contrast, tries to exclude or denigrate the identity of others not like us; to limit or thwart potential relationships; and to impede communication by making our differences seem intolerable. A large portion of the Good News of Jesus to the whole world has to do with acceptance and affirmation. God's Kingdom is a plethora of colors and textures splashed onto the canvas of creation to give us a broad glimpse of His fullness. Or, to change the metaphor, His Kingdom is a symphony of races, cultures and perspectives all joined together in love under the Conductor to make splendid music that pleases Him. (It pleases us, too, if we let it.)

Body Language

How is it that people who are different can come together? Paul's teaching about spiritual gifts, using the analogy of different body parts, has something to say to this issue:

> The body is not made up of one part but of many. If the foot should say, "Because I am not a hand, I do not belong to the body," it would not for that reason cease to be part of the body. And if the ear should say, "Because I am not an eye, I do not belong to the body," it would not for that reason cease to be part of the body. If the whole body were an eye, where would the sense of hearing be? If the whole body were an ear, where would the sense of smell be? But in fact God has arranged the parts in the body, every one of them, just as he wanted them to be. If they were all one part, where would the body be? As it is, there are many parts, but one body.
>
> 1 Corinthians 12:14–20

A phrase in the above passage has a familiar ring to it. Compare verse 18—"God has arranged the parts in the body, every one of them, just as he wanted them to be"—with Acts 17:26: "[God] determined the times set for them and the exact places where they should live."

I don't think it is at all out of context to suggest that this general principle about spiritual gifts can be used in a broader sense. God places spiritual gifts in the Body as He wants them, and He also places the nations of the world as He wants them. Both passages make clear that our diversity is a sovereign act planned and executed by God Himself.

Just as God has assigned gifts and nations where He wants them, Paul goes on to say that we need each other:

> The eye cannot say to the hand, "I don't need you!" And the head cannot say to the feet, "I don't need you!" On the contrary, those parts of the body that seem to be weaker are indispensable, and the parts that we think are less honorable we treat with special honor. And the parts that are unpresentable are treated with special modesty, while our presentable parts need no special treatment. But God has combined the members of the body and has given greater honor

145

to the parts that lacked it, so that there should be no division
in the body, but that its parts should have equal concern for
each other. If one part suffers, every part suffers with it; if one
part is honored, every part rejoices with it. Now you are the
body of Christ, and each one of you is a part of it.

1 Corinthians 12:21–27

Trying to make it alone is like trying to remove parts of our
own bodies. An analogy can be taken only so far, but think of
this passage in terms of the nations represented within the
borders of the United States. If I need the perspective of a
brother or sister from mainland China, who has lived through
the Cultural Revolution or undergone persecution, in order to
gain a bigger picture of God's Kingdom, then how much more
do we in the Church need hundreds or thousands or millions
of brothers and sisters from China? If my Aboriginal mate from
Australia can benefit from my perspective as a Native American on how I can forgive the white man, then how many more
Aboriginals need to hear that message as well?

What happens when one part of the Body says to the other,
"I don't need you"? Imagine a person consisting only of an eye
or a foot. That would not be a person at all! Nor are we the
people of God without each other. God so desires unity in this
crucial body of many nations that I believe He will do all in
His power to make it happen.

Perhaps that is why He is bringing the nations of the world
to America's doorstep. We need to weep with those from
other nations and rejoice with them as well. We need to feel
their pain and they ours. We are not meant to be homogeneous; rather, we are a new body in Christ and a model of
God's love and acceptance for this hurting world.

A Picture from Heaven

When I was in college I started a missions organization
called Cross Cultural Concerns. We began as a prayer group
interceding for missionaries all over the world, but God soon
expanded the vision. We began meeting students from other
countries and asking them what they needed. Most of their
needs were simple: help with the language, assistance in
opening a checking account and other tasks we would con-

sider mundane. My fellow students and I offered what help we could—responding to their requests, inviting these internationals to our apartment-dorms, asking them out to eat and continuing to pray for them as well.

About three or four months into this adventure, God linked me up with some people who had worked with the international student group on campus, and we learned some ways to be more effective. One thing we did was hold special banquets during American holidays. We would invite our international student friends to bring food from their countries, explain their own customs, perhaps demonstrate a cultural dance. Since many of our holidays are focused on God, it was natural for us, in turn, to explain the reason for the celebration. In that way we were able to present the Gospel in an inoffensive way to Muslims from Iraq and Iran, Buddhists from Korea and Thailand, and a whole host of other students from around the world. That year I was able to introduce two internationals to Jesus without leaving my city.

I found something very precious in my time with these foreign friends. I learned things about myself and my own culture just by being with them. I learned, for example, that I take for granted the simplest things around me, and do not even recognize that those elements are part of my own culture. I also learned that, regardless of how different another culture is, we are all just humans with similar needs and desires. It is good to see through the eyes of another. It helps us see ourselves more clearly—we are simple humans, after all—and that an entire world stretches beyond our doorstep; plus it gives us a bigger picture of our God.

In 1998 the Christian drum group from our church was asked to take part in the Second World Christian Gathering of Indigenous People held in Rapid City, South Dakota. (The first had been held two years before in New Zealand, hosted by the Maori.) About a dozen people from our church participated, and I taught a workshop on modeling Native worship and church outreach. It was a Spirit-led time of destiny, as God's mighty warrior peoples from around the world arose to take their places in the Body of Christ.

I will never forget the grand entry as we sat singing at our drum on the platform overlooking the crowd. Maori warriors,

Aboriginals from Australia, Saami from Sweden and Norway, Native Americans from many tribes in full regalia, Africans, South Americans and others joined the processional, dancing and worshiping Jesus together. It was just like a picture from heaven! I tried my best to sing as tears streamed down my face. It was pure beauty, a live demonstration of God's desire as seen at Pentecost, Azusa Street and other places, and a reflection of what the Bride of Christ actually looks like. Now I was seeing God's big vision for myself.

That moment reshaped my life. I will never be the same and can never again settle for less than seeing the greatness of God on earth and His wonderful plan for humanity. Through my encounters with indigenous believers from all over the world, I have learned that God is much bigger than we have ever realized. By oppressing those of another background and keeping them from expressing their faith through their own cultures, the greater Body of Christ has said, "We don't need you. You're not as important as we are." And in essence, when we view our faith through our own myopic vision, we are saying to God, "I don't want to see You for who You really are."

The world is no longer just "out there"; it has come to our doorstep. God has placed people in His Church from all cultures. If one dominates or prohibits the others' expression, then we all suffer. And according to the Scripture, the rest of the Body of Christ in America will never become all we are meant to be unless we include valid expressions from all people groups. In fact, Paul mandates that we treat the lesser members with special honor. As minority churches in America, we are waiting on the dominant churches to recognize our special gifts—and God is waiting to bless you when you do.

I am amazed at the accelerated speed at which God is moving among Native Americans and indigenous peoples around the world. It is just like our Creator to use the weak things of the world to confound the wise. And I believe that our Native American people are finally about to enter a time of true revival, the likes of which the world has never seen!

But I cannot help but wonder: How will the non-Native church receive us?

13

Protocol

RELATING TO GOD, HIS PEOPLE AND HIS LAND

AMERICANS HAVE A LONG HISTORY of bucking the system. In many ways we are actually taught to distrust those in authority. The roots of our rebellion at the civil level go all the way back to the American Revolution. But the religious arena is no different. All religious movements somehow changed after they got to the shores of America and took on their own unique flavor, despite the control attempted by the European religious authorities.

No wonder we Americans have trouble with spiritual authority!

Understanding Authority

Our first key to understanding authority begins with the admission that it is God Himself who has authority over all of creation. When we give credence to His absolute authority to govern the world as well as our lives, we place ourselves in the humble position of submitting to His authority. Submission means we will handle things in God's way and not our own. Only after we submit to His authority can He put us in a position to be *stewards, underrulers* or *keepers* of what is rightfully His domain.

The very first transfer of authority from God to human beings took place in the Garden of Eden, and that responsibility has never been relinquished: "Fill the earth and subdue it. Rule over the fish of the sea and the birds of the air and over every living creature that moves on the ground" (Genesis 1:28).

People in positions of authority will be judged by God, whether they realize it or not, according to how well they managed His domain (see Luke 16:1–11). We are to submit to them, regardless of what their domain happens to be, as long as our submission does not violate one of God's higher laws.

The apostle Paul makes clear that all authority is established by God.

> Everyone must submit himself to the governing authorities, for there is no authority except that which God has established. The authorities that exist have been established by God. Consequently, he who rebels against the authority is rebelling against what God has instituted, and those who do so will bring judgment on themselves. For rulers hold no terror for those who do right, but for those who do wrong. Do you want to be free from fear of the one in authority? Then do what is right and he will commend you. For he is God's servant to do you good. But if you do wrong, be afraid, for he does not bear the sword for nothing. He is God's servant, an agent of wrath to bring punishment on the wrongdoer. Therefore, it is necessary to submit to the authorities, not only because of possible punishment but also because of conscience.
>
> Romans 13:1–5

Over the years certain customs have been developed by different people groups in order to show proper respect. Sometimes we refer to these ways as *acts of protocol.* In Romans 13:7 Paul directs us to "give everyone what you owe him: If . . . respect, then respect; if honor, then honor." Protocol is simply respecting and honoring those to whom respect and honor are due.

Protocol Regarding God

When approaching God, we must observe certain protocol. This is a heart attitude that can be summed up in one word: *humility*. Humility recognizes God and His authority and rightly produces reverent fear about being in the presence of a holy and loving Creator, who is described in Scripture as "a consuming fire" (Hebrews 12:29). In Proverbs 9:10 we are instructed that "the fear of the LORD is the beginning of wisdom, and knowledge of the Holy One is understanding." It is not wise to come before God with a heart attitude of pride, for "God opposes the proud but gives grace to the humble" (James 4:6).

When we approach God, this "protocol of the heart" may take on symbolic gestures, such as bowing our heads, lifting our hands or kneeling. Our reverence is also symbolized in ceremonies such as praying at an altar, anointing with oil or burning cedar. These expressions can all be symbolic reflections of a heart attitude of humility.

Protocol Regarding People

I believe we are to approach people in authority with a similar spirit of humility, exhibiting respect and honor for their places of authority.

A friend of mine had an audience with the Queen of England. Before the meeting, she had to attend a special session on protocol. There are certain patterns, according to British custom, that a person must follow when he or she is in the presence of the ruling monarch. No one can walk up to the Queen, give her a big bear hug and remark, "How's it going, Liz?" Even to initiate shaking her hand or touching her shoulder is considered extremely disrespectful.

Indigenous peoples around the world also have measures of protocol. Over time, manners and customs have been developed that allow us to show respect for those in authority. Native Americans cherish the wisdom of elders, and we honor our elders for this reason. I was taught that when I visit an elder, I should take along a gift to show my respect. It need not be an elaborate gift, just something useful. When calling on elders I have taken groceries, fruit baskets, scarves, even handkerchiefs.

Some forms of protocol among indigenous people are much more involved. A Maori friend from New Zealand explained to me some of the protocol that must be carried out in order to enter a *marai,* a Maori village. In most cases the visiting procession must stop at an appointed place in its approach, and a woman must lead the group with a *karanga,* or call, to the village elders and chief. It must be a woman who makes the first move in order to show the village that the group comes in peace. The ceremony continues with several more customs, until finally the village authorities have welcomed the visitors onto their land. Certain authority is then granted those visitors while they are on Maori land.

Protocol Regarding Land

God has established the authority of host peoples on lands all over the world. Since God Himself made every nation and determined exactly where they should live (see Acts 17:26), each host people is a *keeper* or steward of their particular land. They are responsible to God for what occurs on the land He has entrusted to them.

The Bible sometimes calls those with authority over the land (or other areas of responsibility) "gatekeepers." Dr. Suuqiina, Inupiat author of *Can You Feel the Mountains Tremble?,* describes this spiritual authority:

> Gatekeeping is simply establishing a spiritual immigration policy. Every piece of ground or territory has an entrance and exit place on it. Such places are called the gates of that territory. Every gate has a gatekeeper.
>
> . . . Everyone is a gatekeeper at some level; fathers and husbands are gatekeepers of their households, pastors and elders of their congregations, mayors and council members of their communities. First Nations peoples are gatekeepers of their nations and continents.[1]

152   When the colonists broke from the old countries, they lost many of their traditions. Protocol is not a concept that many

Euro-Americans grasp today, even though it is clearly a scriptural principle. Jesus spoke of Himself in John 10:1–10 as a gatekeeper. He asserted His own authority over His sheep, and condemned as thieves and robbers anyone who tries to enter the sheep pen by some other way.

Whenever I go to a new place to speak, therefore, I try to find out who the tribes are that have been assigned that area by God. I seek to honor them with gifts and to ask their blessing. I also seek the blessings of local pastors (even though most of them have never sought the blessing of the original inhabitants of the land). Such people as these have been granted by God special authority over a land or area of influence.

I would never think of "taking" authority over that which was not given to me with a blessing attached. That is not our Indian way, and I believe ignoring this protocol actually violates our principles as Christians. There is a godly order to everything if we will but follow His ways.

Spiritually Polluted Land

Let me go a little more in depth in the area of authority over land, because this area of protocol affects our lives and ministries more than we realize, and it is often overlooked.

Many pastors and leaders have been praying for revival for years, but it is as though God does not hear their prayers. I wonder how many of these godly men and women have gone to the gatekeepers of their territory, exercised proper protocol and asked to receive permission to be occupying the land? In most cases the land was either stolen outright or bought through trickery from the original inhabitants. In such cases as these, God requires much more from us than simple protocol. When the land is spiritually polluted, we must also go about healing the land according to God's protocol.

Yes, I did say "spiritually polluted." As much as I detest the kind of pollution we see on the roadsides, not to mention oil spills and toxic waste dumps, there is another kind of pollution that has far greater consequences. Consider Ezra's words:

153

"The land you are entering to possess is a land polluted by the corruption of its peoples. By their detestable practices they have filled it with their impurity from one end to the other."

Ezra 9:11

I remember praying with the Cherokee Prayer Initiative at a site in Georgia where there had been a tremendous battle between the Cherokees and the British. According to the records, many lives had been lost there. In one particular area we noticed that the trees were deformed, even gruesome-looking—not just a few trees, but a whole section of the woods. What made them so grotesque-looking? None of us could explain it, but I believe it was a visible result of the battle that had claimed so many lives. When I saw those mangled trees, my mind went to a Scripture:

The creation was subjected to frustration, not by its own choice, but by the will of the one who subjected it, in hope that the creation itself will be liberated from its bondage to decay and brought into the glorious freedom of the children of God. We know that the whole creation has been groaning as in the pains of childbirth right up to the present time.

Romans 8:20–22

For some reason that particular land showed the evidence of its spiritual pollution. I felt as though those trees were indeed crying out to be liberated.

According to the Bible, the earth can be affected by people's sins, and it becomes cursed. Deuteronomy 21:1–9, for example, discusses corporate responsibility for bloodshed in a particular locale. Here are just a few of the hundreds of passages that speak to the issue of spiritually polluted land:

"If my land cries out against me and all its furrows are wet with tears, if I have devoured its yield without payment or broken the spirit of its tenants, then let briers come up instead of wheat and weeds instead of barley."

Job 31:38–40

154

The earth dries up and withers, the world languishes and withers, the exalted of the earth languish. The earth is defiled by its people; they have disobeyed the laws, violated the statutes and broken the everlasting covenant.

Isaiah 24:4–5

How long will the land lie parched and the grass in every field be withered? Because those who live in it are wicked, the animals and birds have perished. Moreover, the people are saying, "He will not see what happens to us."

Jeremiah 12:4

This may be a difficult concept to grasp if you have a Western scientific worldview. Perhaps you are not used to listening to the wind sing to you, or asking the birds to give you wisdom. I have heard Euro-American Bible teachers skip right over many passages dealing with our relationship with the land. Once in a while I even hear the comment, "When the Bible says *the land,* it really means *the people.*" Sorry. I looked it up. *People* means people and *land* means land.

The Scriptures tell us that the land, and every living thing, has a story to tell:

"Ask the animals, and they will teach you, or the birds of the air, and they will tell you; or speak to the earth, and it will teach you, or let the fish of the sea inform you. Which of all these does not know that the hand of the LORD has done this? In his hand is the life of every creature and the breath of all mankind."

Job 12:7–10

It should not seem strange that God has created everything to have a purpose. For millennia indigenous peoples have been learning from what the white man calls "nature," and many of our stories involve animals rather than people. Our remedies for sicknesses were often divinely given to us by certain plants coming to us in our dreams. Through God's divine revelation we have learned how to live in harmony with the land the Creator has given us. I sometimes wonder when the immigrants to this land will learn that it takes a special relationship with God, His creation and the land for all of life to be in balance. Only then can we lay claim to a biblical worldview.

Would you treat your dog differently if you knew you were going to spend eternity with him or her? The writer of Ecclesiastes asks this question: "Who knows if the spirit of man rises upward and if the spirit of the animal goes down into the earth?" (Ecclesiastes 3:21). It appears that God knows the answer; He may even have an eternal plan for Fido!

> The wolf will live with the lamb, the leopard will lie down with the goat, the calf and the lion and the yearling together; and a little child will lead them. The cow will feed with the bear, their young will lie down together, and the lion will eat straw like the ox. The infant will play near the hole of the cobra, and the young child put his hand into the viper's nest.
>
> Isaiah 11:6–8

> I heard every creature in heaven and on earth and under the earth and on the sea, and all that is in them, singing: "To him who sits on the throne and to the Lamb be praise and honor and glory and power, for ever and ever!"
>
> Revelation 5:13

A Comanche elder once told me a story about his early education. When he was small, he said, a missionary came to his parents' home and urged his mother to send him to school. He begged her to allow him to walk to the school the next morning. Finally she agreed. She packed him a lunch and pointed to the woods to the west. "Come back in time to do your chores," she said.

The boy tried to correct his mother. "But the school is to the east."

She persisted in pointing west. So he spent the whole day in the woods and came home just before dark.

"What did you learn today, son?" his mother asked.

"Nothing, Mother. I just sat in the woods all day."

Each day was the same, until about the fourth day, when he answered her differently.

"I saw a rabbit outsmart a fox today, because he could move back and forth more quickly than that fox. Also, I saw a hawk catch a mouse in a field." And he described those dynamics.

156   The reports got longer with each stay in the woods, until the boy began to look forward to the next day with great

excitement. He found himself listening to the wind sing him songs and discovered for himself that everything created has a story to tell.

One morning after several weeks, the mother pointed east. "Only now, son, are you ready to go to school."

Perhaps God looked at the Europeans, who had so much knowledge-based information in that Age of Reason, and seeing that their knowledge was taking them farther and farther away from Him, He led them to peoples who saw things differently. Unfortunately, in those crucial early years of first contact, the Europeans did not learn to add some different ways of thinking to their worldview. Nor does it seem as though things are getting better today.

What Pollutes the Land?

Perhaps God will give us another chance for the worldview of the host peoples and the worldview of the immigrants to be shared before it is too late. In the meantime we should at least understand that our sin does pollute the land and its inhabitants. Dr. Suuqiina points out from Scripture four areas of disobedience that defile the land.[2] I would argue that these very sins have polluted America, some even before the arrival of the white man:

- *Bloodshed* (Numbers 35:33)
- *Sexual immorality* (Leviticus 18:22–28)
- *Broken treaties* (2 Samuel 21:1–14, in which children were held liable for the treaty violation of their father; Isaiah 24:1–6, in which land was defiled by disobedience; and Jeremiah 3:1, in which land was defiled by divorce)
- *Idolatry* (Jeremiah 16:18)

Bloodshed

Native Americans have to plead guilty for blood that was shed on the land before the arrival of the Europeans. Yet I am

157

sure it does not compare with the volume of blood staining the land today.

Sexual Immorality

The sin in America surrounding sexual immorality has taken on a life of its own, including the growing spread of AIDS, unwanted pregnancies and the exponential growth rate of other sexually transmitted diseases. The relationship between sexual immorality and God's judgment on a people was noted by James Adair, a member of the Irish gentry who lived among the Southeastern tribes, during the smallpox epidemic suffered by the Cherokee in 1738. The Cherokees believed that the disease was God's punishment for the increase in adultery among the young married people.[3]

Broken Treaties

The phrase *broken treaties* could summarize the relationship of the U.S. government to Native Americans. Some estimate that there are currently more than eight hundred treaties made by the United States with Native tribes that have not been kept. Others point out that not a single one has been honored fully.

Why would breaking a treaty defile the land? Because a treaty is a covenant, and God takes covenants very seriously.

Idolatry

We do not see a lot of people these days bowing down to carved images, but if we think of idolatry in that limited view, then we are mistaken. Idolatry is any violation of God's first commandment to "have no other gods before me" (Exodus 20:3). A broad definition of "having other gods" would include anything we value more than God Himself.

Certainly one aspect of idolatry is reducing Him to an image that is manageable. In other words, I will believe only those things about God that suit me. This type of idolatry places me in control of who God is. It makes Him compliant with

158

my wishes, not vice-versa. It was this kind of "small-thinking" idol worship that began much of the idolatry in America (and in other places in the world as well).

The dominant society in North America commonly holds that Native Americans were idolaters. Not true. By and large we were a very spiritual people who were almost all monotheistic and whose beliefs were reflected in most aspects of life. The Europeans, by contrast, introduced a compartmentalized view of God so that He could be easily managed—but this created inconsistencies in the Christian lifestyle. To the Indians it seemed that the white man's "god" met them only in church on Sundays. Many believed this "god" was neither great enough to provide unity of belief among the different whites day by day, nor strong enough to enable the whites to live the Gospel message they professed to believe.

One Native chief succinctly described the confusion among the Indians concerning the white man and his "god":

> Brothers, you say there is but one way to worship and serve the Great Spirit. If there is but one religion, why do you people differ so much about it? Why not all agree, as you can all read the same book? . . . Brothers, we are told you have been preaching to the white people in this place. These people are our neighbors. We are acquainted with them. We will wait a little while and see what effect your preaching has upon them. If we find it does them good, makes them honest, less disposed to cheat Indians, we will consider again of what you have said. Brothers, you have now heard our answer to your talk, and this is all we have to say at present. As we are going to part, we will come and take you by the hand, and hope the Great Spirit will protect you on your journey and return you safe to your friends.
>
> Chief Red Jacket, 1805[4]

The Europeans had done an excellent job of contextualizing the Gospel to their own culture—so successful, in fact, that they failed to see the bigness of God around them and in other cultures, including and especially that of their host peoples. The colonists felt their culture reflected God to such a high degree that being a true pilgrim was synonymous with having God's blessing on whatever they chose to do. But the curse from their small-thinking, God-controlling idolatry has never left America. It has plagued the inhabitants of our land in every generation and is still evident today through racism and bigotry—and most often justified with religious verbiage.

Judgments and Blessings on the Land

In his book *Healing the Land: A Supernatural View of Ecology,* author Winkie Pratney points out the ecological judgments and blessings that accompany our disobedience or obedience to God. God's judgments on our disobedience, according to Ezekiel 14, include:

- *Famine* (verse 13)
- *Ecological devastation* (verse 15)
- *War* (verse 17)
- *Disease* (verses 19–20)[5]

We can surely expect Satan to move in on any territory with an atmosphere that welcomes him. We sometimes think of demons as forcing their way in on us, but the idea of demonic intruders is somewhat of a misnomer. An intruder is someone unwelcome. When we abandon our posts as God's good stewards of any area of the Kingdom of God, including territory that formerly welcomed God, we block His needed hand of protection and invite an onslaught of demonic infestation.

The blessings for an obedient nation are much more numerous than the judgments. Pratney's list, based on Leviticus 26, follows (with an additional blessing cited by Suuqiina):

- *Ecological health* (verse 4)
- *Economic health* (verse 5)
- *Personal security* (verse 6a)
- *Civil security* (verse 6b)
- *International security* (verses 7–8a)
- *Honor and growth* (verse 9)
- *Innovation and creativity* (verse 10)
- *God's habitation, not just visitation* (verses 11–12)[6]

I truly believe God is calling His people of all colors and cultures to come together and finally begin to heal the land. As believers who have entered the new millennium, we may find our last opportunity in the twenty-first century to clear the slate of our past sins.

We have long looked at God's Word from a lopsided, monocultural worldview and missed much of its meat. God does not ask for just our prayers; He also charges us to put feet to them. Yet many of the famous passages of the great evangelical stirrings in the past few decades have neglected concern for the land. Look just a bit more closely at two passages of Scripture:

> "When I shut up the heavens so that there is no rain, or command locusts to devour the land or send a plague among my people, if my people, who are called by my name, will humble themselves and pray and seek my face and turn from their wicked ways, then will I hear from heaven and will forgive their sin and *will heal their land.*"
>
> 2 Chronicles 7:13–14 (emphasis added)

> "I looked for a man among them who would build up the wall and stand before me in the gap *on behalf of the land* so I would not have to destroy it, but I found none."
>
> Ezekiel 22:30 (emphasis added)

God aims for the people and the land to be healed. We sometimes forget that the Creator of this earth loves not only the people He made to worship Him, but the land as well. The earth belongs to God; we are just His keepers of it. "The earth is the LORD's, and everything in it, the world, and all who live in it" (Psalm 24:1). But Jeremiah 12:11 prophesied that the land "will be made a wasteland, parched and desolate before me; the whole land will be laid waste *because there is no one who cares*" (emphasis added).

If the believers in this world will not care for God's earth, who will?

14

Getting Beyond "Getting Along"

IF WE WANT TO SEE GOD'S GLORY, it means we are going to actually have to do something about it. Not theorize about it, not just go to another seminar about it, but actively participate in godly actions toward one another. The world offers no lasting solutions to the problems associated with multiculturalism. Temporary hiring practices and teaching about tolerance will last only until the next touchy issue causes us to explode, because they do not change the heart. Tolerant liberals make a show of diversity at socials and cocktail parties, but how many of their children are actually having sleepovers or going on family vacations with one another? Tolerance is simply one step away from bigotry.

For two years I produced, and sometimes hosted, a religious talk show called "House of the Lord." I worked for five organizations—the Catholic Archdiocese of Denver, the Denver Rabbinical Council, the East Denver Ministerial Alliance (most of which were inner-city black churches), the Colorado Council of Churches and Inter-faith Communications International. During that time in my life, God was, at the very least, making sure I learned firsthand the meaning of religious tolerance!

My job as producer was finding areas of interest to all parties concerned and then taping a show using prospective guests and panelists from the varying communities. The nature of the show was always informative and often controversial. We dealt with issues such as immigration policy, capital punishment, nuclear proliferation and sometimes an issue from one particular community. But only on rare occasions would I meet a guest who could go the distance in the area of tolerance. I often heard people of faith make comments about respecting other viewpoints, but those same people tended eventually to reach their saturation point when it came to understanding those who differed from them.

The only thing that will allow us to embrace each other and celebrate our differences is if we can catch a glimpse of God's heart and do it for Him. What better gift can we give back to God than to agree with His plans and live according to His directions? God has a deep and abiding passion for diversity, and He calls us to *celebrate* those differences, not *tolerate* them.

In order to bring about biblical healing, there are at least seven crucial steps we must take:

1. Sincere, devout listening
2. Confession of the wrong done
3. Repentance
4. Forgiveness of the offense
5. Restitution to the appropriate person(s)
6. Healing land that has been defiled
7. Renewed relationships between the parties involved

Let's look briefly at each of these.

1. Listening

I heard once that Mother Teresa was interviewed by a leading TV news reporter. The conversation is reported to have gone something like this.

"Mother Teresa, what do you say to God when you pray?"

"I don't say anything," she answered. "I listen."

That was not the answer the reporter had expected. "Then what does God say?"

She turned to look him directly in the eyes. "He doesn't say anything. He listens."

163

And so must *we* come together to listen. We must listen to the pain. Listen to the guilt. Listen to the years of shame and oppression. And when it is necessary, someone will speak.

Just before Edith and I left Eagle Valley Church in Carson City, Nevada, we held an event called "Search for Healing," directed toward healing the wounds of the elders who had attended Stewart Indian Boarding School. One night we had a "listening banquet" to honor those elders who had suffered senseless pain many years prior. The banquet was hosted by a white church nearby, while another Euro-American church bought the food and did all the preparation and serving. The witness of these two non-Indian churches was in itself a great example of Christ to our Native elders.

There was only one ground rule that evening: Only those who had experienced boarding school could speak. I moderated the evening, and on several occasions had to ask our white friends to please put down their hands.

The meal was great, the service exceptional and the host church incredibly warm. Our elders were treated well by people they would never have thought cared about them. The evening went well, and it set the atmosphere for God to move in a very big way in the areas of confession and reconciliation the following day.

But it can be hard to listen. Those in the dominant society tend to want to move too quickly past the pain, especially when their ancestors were the ones who caused it. I cannot really explain this phenomenon (although I know that dealing with sin is unpleasant), but I have seen it happen many, many times. I have even heard it disguised in religious verbiage, as in one uncomfortable moment when a pastor jumped up to declare, "Let's move on, since we know there is no condemnation to those in Christ Jesus." I am reminded instead of another Scripture: "He who answers before listening—that is his folly and his shame" (Proverbs 18:13).

What the well-meaning folks in the dominant society fail to realize is that our people, and other minorities, have had to live with the pain for dozens, sometimes even hundreds, of years, and our children will have to live with the consequences caused by the very same wounds unless biblical healing takes place. With so much at stake, is it too much to ask that you listen to our stories, given at our own pace, in our own words?

One of the greatest gifts can be listening from the heart when someone else is speaking from the heart. Proverbs 1:5 says, "Let the wise listen and add to their learning." This quality is missing from our fast-paced society, but it is possibly the ultimate sign of respect. Conversely, when our stories are not heard, or when they are disrupted, it is perhaps the ultimate sign of disrespect, and it adds insult to injury.

During my seminary years I was selected to join students from all the religious schools in the Philadelphia area in a course taught through Temple University School of Religion called "Jewish/Christian Dialogue." The Christians represented views ranging from extremely liberal to moderate evangelical. The idea was to expose future rabbis, priests and pastors to other people's thinking, thereby breaking down barriers and creating an atmosphere of mutual appreciation.

After each teaching session, we would gather in small groups to discuss class content and express our opinions and experiences. Regardless of the group, I observed the same tension. The Jewish students needed to express their feelings toward the Christians concerning anti-Semitism and the pain it had caused. But time after time I watched the Christian students deny the pain of the Jewish students. Sometimes their responses even shifted from defensiveness to a bit of anti-Semitism. I hurt for those Jewish students because I saw in their pain the pain of my own people. One lesson I learned from this experience: Until a wounded person can express his pain to a person who represents those who have wounded him, it is very difficult for him to get past it.

But in our quick-fix, instant-message, remote-control, microwave society, we seem to have lost the art of listening to one another. Doctors do not have time to listen to their patients in the ten- to fifteen-minute slots that are scheduled. Parents can barely listen to their children between work, television, dinner preparation and chauffeured trips to soccer practice or ballet. Congregations no longer listen to their pastors when they limit them to a twenty-minute slot once a week to expound God's Word. And people no longer listen to God—for when we pray we usually do not listen.

2. Confession

As a Body we are to make confession one to another: "Confess your sins to each other and pray for each other so that you may be healed" (James 5:16). Sin is against God and ultimately must be taken to Him. We can never substitute forgiveness from each other for God's forgiveness unless He is part and parcel of the equation. But at a human level we were made to confess to one another as well. If we want to bring about healing in our land and among our people, we must learn to confess our wrongs.

As with everything, healing has both a human and a divine dimension. God fully intends for us to go to one another with our hurts and grievances. The remedy for anger on a brother-to-brother level—and I believe this principle includes anger against ethnic groups as well—is set forth by Jesus:

> "If you are offering your gift at the altar and there remember that your brother has something against you, leave your gift there in front of the altar. First go and be reconciled to your brother; then come and offer your gift."
>
> Matthew 5:23–24

God considers the act of confession and reconciliation so important that without it, our worship is actually rejected by God. The gift remains at the altar until the wound is taken care of; only then does God accept our act of worship.

John Dawson, founder of the International Reconciliation Coalition, suggests that we all do an inventory. As you go to your altar of prayer, consider your own life and identity, including ethnicity, culture and family. Have you ever asked yourself, *Does anyone out there, including those from other ethnicities and cultures, have anything against me or the people I represent?*

By now you may be asking if this means you are supposed to go to every person you see who may have been offended by your particular ethnic group, and ask for their forgiveness. Though this may seem a silly question, I have been asked it before. We do not live our faith in a vacuum. Just as we do not share the Gospel with every person we see, but only those to whom God leads us, so we do not engage in this kind of confession and healing with every person we see. God calls us to use wisdom. Not everyone will be receptive to our message, and an insensitive approach will drive people further from Jesus Christ rather than toward Him.

But God does work through our relationships and His divine appointments in our lives to bring others to Christ. And as we follow the leading of the Holy Spirit, He will lead us to confession and healing with our brothers and sisters.

When the directive is clear in our hearts that we must confess sin and reconcile with another individual, Jesus warns us concerning our tendency to procrastinate:

> "Settle matters quickly with your adversary who is taking you to court. Do it while you are still with him on the way, or he may hand you over to the judge, and the judge may hand you over to the officer, and you may be thrown into prison. I tell you the truth, you will not get out until you have paid the last penny."
>
> Matthew 5:25–26

We are wise to settle problems between ourselves rather than wait and be handed over to the judge. The principle is that God's judgment for unresolved issues and sins will be more severe and exacting if we do not take care of these ourselves.

Because of the involvement of the Anglican Church of Canada in certain atrocities associated with the Canadian Residential Schools (similar to the U.S. Government Indian Boarding Schools), many lawsuits have been brought by former students. Charges include sodomy, rape, even manslaughter, and tie the Anglican Church in as a culpable agent for these incidents, some of which occurred almost a century ago. A bishop friend tells me it is possible, incredible as it sounds, that the denomination may go bankrupt as a result of these lawsuits. The Church made an official apology to the indigenous peoples of Canada, but her action and efforts may have been too little, too late.

A severe judgment, indeed! There are many wounds here and around the world that have not yet been healed. God expects us to settle them ourselves, before He has to.

167

3. Repentance

Repentance is an attitude of the heart expressed in both words and actions. We often substitute confession for repentance, but biblically that is dead wrong. Repentance means to turn in the opposite direction. John the Baptist's words to the cynical Pharisees and Sadducees are essential for our day: "Produce fruit in keeping with repentance" (Matthew 3:8). When it comes to dealing with touchy issues, our sinful attitudes seek to exclude us from responsibility, but an attitude of righteousness takes the blame.

Is it possible for an individual to make a difference concerning the wrongs done to a nation or people group? The answer is yes.

John Dawson has coined a phrase that helps us understand the dynamic at work: *identificational repentance.* Quite simply this means that we can repent, by identifying with one race or culture, to a person of another race or culture against which ours has perpetrated injustice. Because we are all guilty of like-minded thoughts or actions, we are able to stand before God, identify with the sins of our particular race or culture, and seek forgiveness from Him and from the ones who have been hurt. Jesus told us that if we even *think* a sin in our hearts, we are guilty of that sin, so it should be easy for us to relate to the sins of others. And through identificational repentance we are answering God's call to "stand before me in the gap" (Ezekiel 22:30).

The Bible is full of examples of those who identified with the sins of others (including their forefathers): Moses, Ezra, Job, Nehemiah, Daniel and Stephen. Even the Lord Jesus Christ, by dying in our place, identified with us: "God made him who had no sin to be sin for us, so that in him we might become the righteousness of God" (2 Corinthians 5:21). We are all called to join Him in this Christlike activity.

God still looks for people to stand in the gap in order to heal the land and the people. The land will not be healed without confession, repentance, restitution and restoration by the blood of Jesus. God looks to believers (not unbelievers) to meet the conditions and bring that about. We are called a "royal priesthood" (1 Peter 2:9), which means that, as priests, we are to talk to God about the sins of the people and offer sacrifices for them. We are to apply the blood of Jesus to the wounded situations of our world.

In 1997 God asked me to hold a festival for racial reconciliation. I had little idea what it would entail. At first I thought it would be a time of Native American and European-American healing surrounding the boarding school issues. It grew to be much more than that. God dug deep into my heart to bring out some attitudes I had not recognized or noticed in a long time. And when it came time to choose someone to offer a statement of repentance to the African-American community, God said to me, "You will do it."

I was already planning, coordinating, hosting and moderating the whole event. I had plenty to do. But His words to me were fixed.

I would like to include here the statement I gave that day—not because it is great (it is not) or because I am proud of it (I am not). I want to use this statement because in order to come up with it, I had to break down the gates of pride in my own heart and feel the shame of hundreds of years of prejudice, in order to bring forth repentance in a way that would please the Father. I would also like to quote it because since that time of self-examination, my once-hidden attitudes have changed from my heart and have affected my actions toward African-Americans in a tremendously positive way. My statement is both true and sincere. Please forgive me if it offends you.

I started out by quoting Nehemiah's prayer of identificational repentance before God:

> "O LORD, God of heaven, the great and awesome God, who keeps his covenant of love with those who love him and obey his commands, let your ear be attentive and your eyes open to hear the prayer your servant is praying before you day and night for your servants, the people of Israel. I confess the sins we Israelites, including myself and my father's house, have committed against you. We have acted very wickedly toward you. We have not obeyed the commands, decrees and laws you gave your servant Moses."
>
> Nehemiah 1:5–7

169

Then I said:

Nehemiah confessed the sins of the Israelites, himself and his ancestors, even though he had never lived in his own country. He grew up in exile. He had no human reason to confess those sins—yet God led him to. Today I stand here before you very much like Nehemiah, identifying with the sins that mixed-blood Cherokees and others have committed against African-Americans.

They say one of the noblest traits of the Cherokee people is to adapt—to take what we want from the greater society and use it for ourselves. As a Cherokee Indian I confess that our people, one of the "civilized" tribes, enslaved African peoples just like our white neighbors. We adapted. As a mixed-blood Cherokee I confess that it was those with the same mixed blood who acted out of greed to enslave African-Americans in order to gain land, to improve on a selfish lifestyle for ourselves at others' great expense and detriment. We pursued the very same spirit of greed that caused us to lose our own homeland. Perhaps it was the judgment of God against us.

Unlike our Seminole neighbors, we and other tribes did not incorporate our slaves into our tribes, but after they had crossed the same Trail of Tears as we had, bled the same blood through injury, lost the same toes and fingers through frostbite, starved the same hunger, left their same loved ones in shallow ditches by the roadside, instead we separated you into a lower class in Oklahoma. We denied you the right to your own land, and we refused to give you citizenship—a struggle that is still active to this day.

As a mixed-blood man who readily enjoys the benefits of white society, I confess that our people have greatly sinned against all African-Americans. The American slave trade was one of the ugliest blights in history, and as a nation whose stated desire was to reflect Christ, we sorely failed. From the cruelty of capturing Africans and forcibly removing you from your homeland; to the completely inhumane conditions on the slave ships; to the constant separation and destruction of your families; to the constant rape of African-American women and the emasculation of your men; to the treatment of African-Americans as equal to an investment of property or animals, some valued less, some valued more, but none valued as human beings created in God's image—I repent.

The American slave trade must be one of the greatest stenches in the nostrils of God in history. Those who lived in other parts of the country than the South tolerated this sin for too long because often they benefited from it. The same spirit of greed was present to allow this cruelest of cruelties to continue.

As a son of the South my roots go deep into a line of people who lived and fought to keep your people as slaves. My own grandfather used the term *Negra,* a term left over from slavery. My own grandmother, though she midwived many African-American babies into this world, and though she fed anyone who was hungry, regardless of color, would not sit at the same table as a black person.

I confess that in my own family there are at least five generations of slave-owners. As I read documents from the past, I see entries of family members, such as my sixth-generation great-grandfather, "Jacob Woodley appointed as juror," on the same page that I see that "Thomas a slave, convicted of housebreaking, ears cropped and given 39 lashes." And "James a slave, convicted of larceny, stealing one silver coin—hung by the neck until dead." As in the words of Jeremiah, I and my fathers have sinned.

Yet it is the tens of thousands of unwritten pages—the pages recorded in God's record book of human history—that haunt my conscience the most, and that I believe still plague America today. It is the long history of cruelty after slavery that has quenched the Spirit of God in America. The slavery has not stopped. It is still going on.

I must confess before God and you that I have walked a little faster and held onto my child's hand a little more tightly simply because a black man was approaching. I confess my prejudice. How many times at sports or entertainment events have I chosen to sit away from a section of African-Americans, at the same time highly esteeming black sports and entertainment figures? I confess my hypocrisy. How many times have I been in a convenience store paying for gas when a group of young black men walked in and the quick thought ran through my mind, *Is there a chance that this will be a robbery?* I confess my self-absorption. Yes, the slavery continues, but it is we, the rest of society, who are enslaved.

We are enslaved to denying the sins of our fathers. We are enslaved to the repression of our own prejudice and racial sins. We are enslaved to the myth of sameness and comfort—an affront to God's wonderful diversity. I commend to you that our sins are so many and so filthy that only God could forgive the depths of them. Greed, hatred, racism, prejudice, selfishness, enmity, strife, hardened hearts and, above all else, idolatry. It is humanly impossible for you, my beautiful black friends, to forgive such atrocities.

On behalf of those who choose to identify with these intolerable, detestable sins, as a mixed-blood Cherokee, as a son of the South, as an American citizen who has sinned greatly against you and all African-Americans and, most importantly, against God, I ask, I beg you, to ask God to help you forgive me and forgive us, your brothers and sisters, for our sins are many. We also ask forgiveness from a merciful God.

Perhaps you thought to yourself while reading my ugly sins, *How could a man who feels such prejudice write a book about embracing multiculturalism?* I asked God the same question. But I believe it is because I have seen the ugliness that resides in my own heart and in the hearts of my good Christian family that I needed to write a book such as this. You see, I have a human condition; it is called sin. In my sinfulness I will ignore those who are different from myself, just to avoid looking at myself too long and too hard.

Because of my own bad heart, I recognize these same attitudes in others—preachers, Sunday school teachers, prophets, it does not matter. We all suffer from the propensity toward sameness. I wrote this book because I need you, whatever your shade or custom, to keep my own heart in check. I need to live and love in the family God has made in order to be secure in my own identity. And I need you in order to please our heavenly Father.

But how shall we who are such grievous sinners continue to come together?

4. Forgiveness

It is part of God's great nature of mercy that when sincere confession of sin is made, those who have been offended do not have a right to withhold forgiveness, any more than God Himself does. In fact, to follow God in obedience, the offended party must *bless* the offender: "Love your enemies, do good to those who hate you, bless those who curse you, pray for those who mistreat you" (Luke 6:27–28). Jesus' words are echoed and amplified by Paul: "Do not repay anyone evil for evil. Be careful to do what is right in the eyes of everybody. If it is possible, as far as it depends on you, live at peace with everyone" (Romans 12:17–18).

Jesus insists that we forgive our brothers every time we have the opportunity, regardless of the offense and regardless of how often it occurs—"not seven times, but seventy-seven times" (Matthew 18:22). The basis for this command is simple: We have been forgiven by God, who has given us life, and in every way has acted in our best interest. He who has every right to exercise unforgiveness toward His children seeks only to forgive. We, too, then, must forgive the lesser crimes that our brothers and sisters have committed against us. To do anything less would seize a prerogative that even God Himself does not exercise.

The consequences for us, if we do not forgive with all sincerity, are grave. In Jesus' story of the two debtors, the lesser debtor, who would not forgive, was "turned . . . over to the jailers to be tortured, until he should pay back all he owed. This is how my heavenly Father will treat each of you unless you forgive your brother from your heart" (Matthew 18:34–35).

5. Restitution

If you steal my car, and a year later you come to me and ask for my forgiveness, one of the things I will ask you is, "Where is my car?" If you fail to consider my loss, then I will be inclined to question your sincerity. But God is very sincere about restitution. Israel suffered under Egypt for 430 years. Not only did He free them, but He caused their very oppressors to finance their freedom. He told Moses: "'Tell the people that men and women alike are to ask their neighbors for articles of silver and gold.' (The LORD made the Egyptians favorably disposed toward the people . . .)" (Exodus 11:2–3).

173

Why is restitution necessary? Because it is commanded by God, so obedience calls for it.

Restitution does several things, as I understand it, to advance the healing process. First, it leaves a visible testimony so others can see that the injustice has been settled. Second, it clears the offender's conscience from any further guilt. Paul stated, "I strive always to keep my conscience clear before men and God" (Acts 24:16). An unclear conscience is a dangerous thing (see 1 Timothy 1:19)!

Too often the results of confession and repentance and even the receipt of forgiveness without restitution are continued guilt and regrets. Without restitution a stumblingblock of offense and injustice remains in the path for others to trip over. Once restitution has been made, however, we open the door for God to release joy and freedom for both parties, and for a tangible legacy to give testimony to the Lord's goodness for future generations.

The Old Testament principle of repayment—that which has been taken, plus twenty percent—seems to be the standard God expects:

> The LORD said to Moses: "If anyone sins and is unfaithful to the LORD by deceiving his neighbor about something entrusted to him or left in his care or stolen, or if he cheats him, or if he finds lost property and lies about it, or if he swears falsely, or if he commits any such sin that people may do— when he thus sins and becomes guilty, he must return what he has stolen or taken by extortion, or what was entrusted to him, or the lost property he found, or whatever it was he swore falsely about. He must make restitution in full, add a fifth of the value to it and give it all to the owner on the day he presents his guilt offering."
>
> Leviticus 6:1–5

The only specific mention of restitution in the New Testament is Zacchaeus' statement to Jesus. Rather than the standard twenty percent, the tax collector was willing to pay back four times the amount he had stolen (see Luke 19:8). I'll bet the neighbors could not wait for Jesus to go home that day so they could receive Zacchaeus at their front doors! Jesus was so impressed by the new convert's generosity that He said to him, "Today salvation has come to this house, because this man, too, is a son of Abraham" (Luke 19:9).

The point was not that Zacchaeus' generosity saved him, but that his sudden sense of justice showed evidence of his salvation, just as works in the epistle of James demonstrate faith. So, too, our enthusiasm to make restitution for wrongs done shows evidence of our salvation and displays our faith.

I truly believe that any reconciliation effort runs the danger of falling short when restitution is overlooked. To dismiss the biblical principle of restitution as implausible goes against God's intention and commandment. If we do not consider restitution, we automatically close the door for God to work according to His will and Word.

To whom and by whom should restitution be made? First, to the person or people who have suffered the wrong. Those who have been beneficiaries as a result of the injustice should be the ones making restitution. Scripture suggests the "kinsman-redeemer" or "next-of-kin" rule (see Ruth 3:12). It makes sense to follow the closest line of contact between those who have suffered wrong and those who should repay.

Concerning restitution I usually ask myself a few questions:

1. Who (or whose ancestors) were actually involved in the injustice?
2. Has the person making restitution (or his or her ancestors) gained in any way as a result of the injustice being addressed?
3. Has the person to whom restitution is being made (or his or her ancestors) suffered loss in any way from the injustice that is being addressed?

If the appropriate person cannot be found to fulfill the "kinsman-redeemer" principle, then the Bible says restitution should be made to the Lord via the priest:

> "When a man or woman wrongs another in any way and so is unfaithful to the LORD, that person is guilty and must confess the sin he has committed. He must make full restitution for his wrong, add one fifth to it and give it all to the person he has wronged. But if that person has no close relative to

whom restitution can be made for the wrong, *the restitution belongs to the* LORD *and must be given to the priest,* along with the ram with which atonement is made for him."
Numbers 5:5–8 (emphasis added)

These days "the priest" could mean churches or ministries that are somehow related to the victims of the injustice. For example, in a case in which whites are making restitution to blacks, it would be right, if the "kinsman-redeemer" principle cannot be followed, for black churches or ministries to end up as the beneficiaries.

In the modern reconciliation movement, restitution is often the forgotten commandment. It is the spirit of the age to consider the loss of the victim as trivial, his "hard luck," and not to provide restitution. Yet the Scripture leaves no room whatsoever to omit acts of restitution. Biblical restitution may begin with words and tokens, but it must always lead to more substantive actions (taking into consideration the ability of the person making restitution), such as the return of goods, monetary payment, services and the return of lands.

6. Healing the Land

As I stated in the previous chapter, God has a vested interest in our healing the land. Again, to many people this may seem somewhat bizarre, but as human beings we have cursed the land, and we are the ones who must pronounce its redemption in Christ.

Notice the biblical basis for this. Deuteronomy 27:15–26 lists curses that would befall Israel if she turned aside from God's commands. Some Christians believe that all curses were lifted at Calvary. While it is true that the blood of Jesus potentially lifts all curses, and that "Christ redeemed us from the curse of the law by becoming a curse for us" (Galatians 3:13), it is not until the end of the story, at the consummation of all things, that the final curse is lifted. "No longer will there be any curse. The throne of God and of the Lamb will be in the city, and his servants will serve him" (Revelation 22:3).

In his book *Healing America's Wounds,* John Dawson points out from Deuteronomy 27 the many ways that nations

bring curses on themselves by participating in sins like idolatry and injustice. He believes the weight of the curse is not
necessarily the presence of the demonic but the absence of
God's favor:

> In one sense, the curse of God could be seen as the absence
> of God's needed favor. . . . It is not that God abdicates His gov-
> ernance of one square inch of this planet. His pursuing grace
> continues. "Where sin abounded, grace did much more abound"
> (Romans 5:20, kjv). But His presence is veiled. "Thou hast cov-
> ered thyself with a cloud, that our prayer should not pass
> through" (Lamentations 3:44, kjv). Much more terrifying than
> the presence of the adversary is the curse that results when the
> Lord turns His face away from us. . . . Our prime objective,
> therefore, in intercession and spiritual warfare is not the
> removal of the enemy, but the return of the glory. The restora-
> tion of God's needed favor.[1]

I hope we are coming to a place in our history where we
recognize that we need God's favor in the affairs of this country. One of the results of the absence of the glory of God in
our land has been a rejection of the Creator in favor of polytheistic spirituality, non-theistic spirituality and situational
ethics. It is as though a spirit of delusion has been sent to dupe
us. Often it is difficult to get the unbelieving world to take
the true God seriously.

Stephen Carter observes in his noted work *The Culture of
Disbelief: How American Law and Politics Trivialize Religious Devotion:*

> In contemporary American culture, the religions are more
> and more treated as just passing beliefs—almost fads, older,
> stuffier, less liberal versions of the so-called New Age—rather
> than as the fundamentals upon which the devout build their
> lives. . . . And if religions *are* fundamental, well, too bad—at
> least, if they're the wrong fundamentals, if they're incon-
> venient, give them up! If you can't remarry because you have
> the wrong religious belief, well, hey, believe something else!
> If you can't take your exam because of a Holy Day, get a new
> Holy Day! If the government decides to destroy your sacred
> lands, just make some other lands sacred! . . . And through all
> this trivializing rhetoric runs the subtle but unmistakable

177

message: pray if you like, worship if you must, but whatever you do, do not on any account take your religion seriously.[2]

Perhaps the atmosphere that allows God to be trivialized is a blessing in disguise. The Church often seems to do well when she is a minority. If those of us who take God seriously could close the ranks of our many divisions, I believe God would be pleased and return His needed favor to our land. Part of this process involves healing God's land and restoring it to His intended purposes.

7. Renewed Relationships

By the time I was graduated from high school, my three older siblings were spread across the country and, later, across the world. My mother has often worried about the great distances we live from each other. If she were to die and her children never gathered together again, she would consider it a great tragedy, perhaps even her failure in life.

Why? Because my mother has a heart for her children. Even though she enjoys us individually, she thinks there is something special about the four of us getting together and enjoying each other's presence. Sure, we are grown up, we have spouses and children, and some of our children have children. That makes it even more special. In my mom's eyes, we were always meant to be a family.

I believe that is how God sees His children as well. Our different colors, cultures, experiences and worldviews make it even more special when we come together. But because we have not celebrated our differences, we have suffered misunderstanding. These have led to tragedies in our own country and around the world. Some of these tragedies are atrocities centuries old, the wounds of which have never healed. To God, who is not bound by time, unrepented sin is still a cause of offense, and it creates a welcome sign to the enemy to "come and occupy."

In my first year of pastoring on a reservation in Nevada, we began to build up the children's church by driving the van to another reservation and picking up kids. When we were up to about thirty children, however, some of the kids "suddenly" remembered that they did not like one of the families present at our church. (It would not surprise me if the parents had reminded them.) From that point on we would have half the children one Sunday and the other half the next. When one group found out that the other group was on the van, the first group would choose to stay home.

I visited the kids and some of the parents to find out what the feud was about. There were plenty of accusations back and forth, but each was in retaliation, so they said, for what the others had done before. I was finally able to trace the root of this Indian version of the Hatfields and McCoys down to a disruption that had occurred between the families several decades earlier. None of the children had any knowledge of the original incident and probably still do not today. Yet they continue the fight.

When sin, including but not limited to injustice, is not dealt with, it does not fizzle out and die like a Fourth of July sparkler. It collects more injustice (or idolatry or whatever) like additional sparklers, and ends up lighting up the sky. Nor does a serious wound, left untreated, heal itself. It gets infected and painful and eventually even draws parasites. Unconfessed sin only breeds more sin.

It is time for the Body of Christ to come together and heal our wounds. We must not come together as enemies, ready to place blame. This will not please our heavenly Father, and it will only produce more wounds. No, we must treat our wounds as injuries that have occurred within the family.

Nor can we come together hiding the truth, hiding the pain or hiding the consequences of the wounds we have suffered. This would not please our Maker, for He will meet with us only when we come together in honorable, visceral truth. But if we do not speak the truth in love, we are only peeling away another layer of the onion, and it will sting our eyes and invite the enemy in.

In 1 John 3:18 the apostle said, "Dear children, let us not love with words or tongue but with actions and in truth." If I am part of perpetuating a system of injustice toward a person or people group, I need to think through the ramifications. I must ask myself how my actions have affected those who

179

have suffered because of the injustice. Then I need to act in the opposite spirit in each area of my life.

I need to listen to my brothers and sisters. I need to repent, being willing to loosen the many strands of iniquity that cling to me and others like the tentacles of an octopus. I need to forgive, when appropriate, and to ask and receive the forgiveness of others. Then I need to make restitution for systems that continue to breed oppression and injustice. Only then will I clear the way for the healing of the land and enjoy renewed relationships of joy with all my brothers and sisters.

15

What Does the Kingdom Look Like?

"My prayer is not for them alone. I pray also for those who will believe in me through their message, that *all of them may be one,* Father, just as you are in me and I am in you. May they also be in us so that the world may believe that you have sent me. I have given them the glory that you gave me, that *they may be one* as we are one: I in them and you in me. May they be brought to *complete unity* to let the world know that you sent me and have loved them even as you have loved me."

John 17:20–23 (emphasis added)

JESUS' WORDS OF PETITION to the Father ring with the call for true unity—the kind He and the Father have. Jesus seems to be declaring in His prayer that if His followers come into this kind of unity, the world will believe and know that God sent Him. We already know what happens conversely: When we are not in unity, it causes the world to doubt and disbelieve, and real people suffer an eternity without Jesus.

I wonder what standard of judgment God will use to judge those of us who have kept people away from Jesus because of our prejudice and cultural bias?

The Kingdom of God is growing slowly in the area of unity in diversity. Unfortunately, some of the multicultural

181

churches I have observed are not actually celebrating the differences but learning to tolerate them. Instead of exploring the vast treasure God has given them, they are learning to make the necessary concessions, more or less, to keep everyone happy. Too bad—although this is at least a start.

This is not to say that there are not stellar examples of churches celebrating our diversity, but they are few and far between. A few instances do stick out in my mind that can be used as metaphors to describe the multicultural Kingdom of God. But every now and then something so dramatic occurs in the area of unity and diversity that it brings incredible glory to God, brings new believers into the Kingdom and dismantles Satan's schemes and causes him to regroup. The 1995 Promise Keepers Clergy Conference in Atlanta was such a time.

Shouldering One Another

More than forty thousand ministers gathered from what seemed like every ethnic group and culture in the world. I applaud Promise Keepers for giving God the freedom to use such a great opportunity, without letting it slip by, to demonstrate Kingdom unity. Coach Bill McCartney, founder of the organization, took the microphone at one point in that massive sports arena and began to recognize the Native Americans present. From there he broadened the welcome and made confession of sin to all people of color who were present. In the midst of this conciliatory effort, the coach called for all people of color to come forward in order to be honored.

As a few began making their way down the aisles, spontaneous applause broke out from the white ministers. Suddenly leaders throughout the arena began to embrace one another and confess to one another past racism and acts of prejudice. Everyone was crying, some profusely. A spirit of humility engulfed the place as I have never experienced. Here were grown men casting away macho pride and crying like babies while they forgave and embraced one another.

This holy pandemonium went on for some time, and every so often you could hear McCartney's voice over the crowd, saying, "Keep coming up to the platform, we want to honor you," and, "Make way in the aisles."

The honoring was already taking place among people all over the arena, but some of the men were still trying to follow the instructions and make their way to the front. It was then that I noticed an older African-American man with a cane trying to manage his own way down the aisle behind me. What happened next literally brought me to my knees. It was one of those moments when time seemed to stand still—the kind of moment you saw on the covers of *Life* magazine. I doubt that anyone was taking pictures at that moment, but I know God took a snapshot of it, and it is framed in heaven for eternity.

There was more than gray hair about this African-American elder that gave him dignity. Although his limp was obvious, he walked with a determination that said resolutely, "I have suffered a lifetime of prejudice, and I have been waiting all my life to see this day. Now it is here and I will accept your apology." Unfortunately the man could not make headway because of all the people milling in the aisle.

Then I noticed that I was not the only person watching the black elder. He had also drawn the attention of two elderly white men. I watched, as if in slow motion, as those two white men made their way to the black elder. If I had to guess, I would say all three were World War II veterans. When they reached him, they shook his hand and gave him a hug. Then I saw them ask him something. I knew what was about to happen—and it did.

The two elderly white gentlemen began to hoist the black man with the cane up onto their shoulders. As they did, the crowd began to part. Amid the tears and applause in our small area, the men began to move slowly down the aisle toward the front of the arena. As far as I could see, people made a way for them.

I do not know if they made it to the front of the auditorium, but from the look on the face of that sage old African-American man, I would say the honor had already taken place. Just as apparent was the joy of the two white men who carried him. They showed without hesitation the servant heart of their Savior.

There were probably many great moments that occurred in the huge auditorium that day during that landmark event. But I will always be grateful to have been in the area I was, to witness one simple act of humility and grace.

What does the Kingdom look like? It looks like that.

Host People's Gifts

Have you ever noticed that many of the characteristics of different people groups seem to reflect the land on which they live? Perhaps it could just as well be the land reflecting the people. Whatever the case, I know there is a connection.

Earlier in the book I mentioned the Second World Christian Gathering of Indigenous People held in Rapid City, South Dakota, in 1998. One of the blessings I took away from this spectacular event was a deeper appreciation of the gifts God has bestowed on other peoples of the world. This event provided many snapshots for me of the Kingdom of God. It was as if a special, unique gifting from God to each indigenous people became palpable.

When my friends David Kahiapo and Leon Siu began singing the songs of their native Hawaii, the atmosphere of the large auditorium seemed to take on a mood of unfettered beauty. I was entranced (although I have enjoyed Hawaii only from pictures). As the other Hawaiians shared their *hula*, it was as if God had placed us once again in the Garden of Eden. That is when it hit me. Perhaps Hawaii is one of the reminders that God has left on this earth to remind us of the innocent beauty of the Garden that He once planned for us! The native Hawaiians present were gracious, beautiful and had a sweetness to their disposition. Their whole essence seemed to reflect the *aloha* aspect of God and the islands He has given them.

Equally enchanting, in yet another way, were the Maori from New Zealand. The warrior spirit in me arose as I watched the Maori do their *haka* (war dance), and they made me want to be militant for Jesus. It reminded me that Yahweh is a warrior and not to be trifled with. Watching the Maori reminded me that, as a Church, we are already victorious over the enemy, and that we need to be aggressive in taking back all ground we have lost to Satan.

In the Aboriginal peoples from Australia, I saw simplicity of faith, and I thought of how we often make things too complicated when we approach God. I cannot imagine any people living on the Australian continent other than the Aboriginal peoples. They and the land have grown together to become one.

In the Samoans I saw the joy of the Lord and His radical presence. In the Saami people of Norway and Sweden, I saw God's honesty, innocence and acceptance.

As each group was highlighted, it was as if the Lord was saying, "Do you see the wonderful gifts I have given the peoples of this world? These gifts are to be shared, so that you all may be one."

An overwhelming spirit of perfect unity in diversity was present during those ten days, and I will always be grateful for the experience.

John Dawson has led the way in causing the Body of Christ to think of the ethnic giftings that accompany the people of each particular land. I have heard John ask if the particular giftings of each people group might be a reflection of an aspect of the personality of God. Dawson also believes that these giftings can be passed on as blessings from the host people of the land to its immigrants.

If this is the case—and I believe it is—then, as with every gift, there is accompanying responsibility. Gifts from God are to be shared, not hoarded or perverted. God knew our appointed times and boundaries (see Acts 17:26), and He intended for the good cultural giftings of the Native peoples of North America to be shared with humble immigrants, ready to receive their many gifts of identity and hospitality.

In many cases, however, the immigrants could not receive those gifts because they were not teachable, and thus they missed out on much of God's plan. Chief Powhatan, of Pocahontas fame, once asked the new immigrants, "Why do you take by force that which you would have easily been given in love?"

At other times the host peoples were hostile and violent, giving great cause for offense and holding back their giftings and God's intended blessing.

Today God is calling forth the ethnic giftings of all people groups in order to express His glory. In these expressions, and through the "marriage" of the various expressions, God wants to accomplish His will. No one group can adequately express God's grandeur. The result of forced homogeneity is spiritual and cultural desolation.

Immigrant People's Gifts

If the host peoples possess wonderful giftings from God, what about those of European descent who have immigrated into other native lands around the world? Can their unique giftings come to light after so much destruction has already been wrought?

I watched a television interview with a woman who was a traditional Mohawk elder. She was pointing out the simplicity of her people and explaining that they did not need all the trappings of modern society. Then she turned to the reporter, grinning sheepishly.

"But them airplanes," she said. "That's a pretty good thing, I have to admit."

The technology that Europeans brought to our shores may have brought with it problems, yet not many of us would want to live without it. Perhaps American ingenuity and perseverance coupled with Native American values would have compensated for the negative aspects of modern technology. Consider this recent "synergy" between the Salish and Kootanai tribes and the Montana Department of Highways.

Highway 93 runs right through the Flathead Indian Reservation—in my opinion, some of the most beautiful country on earth. The state of Montana wants to expand this highway, the busiest and most dangerous in the state, to four lanes in order to make it safer, but there are problems. Biologists agree that a four-lane would destroy too much wildlife. Easier access would lead to more development of areas that are already overpopulated. The state wants to keep up with the fast-paced majority culture and promote tourism, but the Salish and Kootanai tribes want to maintain a more serene lifestyle and be responsible stewards of the earth and wildlife.

With such diametrically opposed values, could there be any solution? There is, in an example that shows the genius of the Creator's plan when the immigrant and host peoples decide to work in equal partnership.

There will be a four-lane highway through the reservation, but "the design of the reconstructed highway," according to the plan, "is premised on the idea that the road is a visitor and that it should respond to and be respectful of the land and the Spirit of Place."[1] The new road will not cut the normal gashes through hills and earth; it will follow the contours of the landscape. To safeguard wild animals and prevent collisions, engineers are designing at least 42 wildlife crossings under and over the highway, including one for grizzly bears. Officials say it may be the first wildlife overpass to be constructed in the United States. The leaders have also agreed to work together toward a solution for minimizing overpopulation.

One unexpected benefit of this synergy: Engineers believe that the addition of passing lanes, turning lanes, climbing lanes and wider shoulders will make the road safer for drivers—the original purpose, after all!

At this time of unprecedented population growth, if we do not deal with the old problems as well as the new ones that arise daily, we will poison the air and water for everyone, including for the future generations we hold dear. Together we can find solutions if we learn to appreciate the giftedness in one another.

The white people brought with them many other gifts, too. And according to God's ingenious plan, He uses what was meant for evil in our land and brings good from it.

I think again of Moses, who was abandoned at birth to a seemingly unknown destiny. Things in Egypt could not have looked much darker for the captive Israelites. Yet in God's sovereign plan, Moses ended up being raised in the household of the very leader who had tried to kill him and who was enslaving Moses' people. Even though Pharaoh provided Moses with food, clothing, money, education and all he had, God's purposes called Moses to a better day.

It seems to me that God set about not only to free the Israelites but also to spare Egypt. He began His judgments with minor catastrophes, which progressively became worse.

I also believe God has used American immigrants in a strange sort of way to sustain us as Native people. It is strange, because the same government that tried to wipe us out now provides the Indian community with many basic necessities. Like Moses, Native Americans are beginning to cry out for God's plan and for His intended freedom.

On a spiritual level there is a tidal wave of non-Native intercessors praying around the world for Native giftings to come forth in order to heal our land, both physically and spiritually. In the past Europeans have not generally had the knack for talking to trees or commanding curses to depart. Because America was given to Native Americans, our involvement is required to restore the land. The same is true of other indigenous peoples in other countries around the world.

White Americans add the giftings of their own Old World cultures to the mix. While God never intended to create another England in America, He wanted the giftings of that nation's people to blend with the Native American giftings. Each ethnic mix, added to the other in God's way, only serves to enhance the gifts of all the rest.

Perfect Partnership: Us and God

God is looking for host and immigrant peoples alike to partner together to do His will. Combining the strengths of several groups creates what is known today as synergy. The idea is that more can be accomplished together than separately. For this to happen, there must be true partnership in the faith. God always calls His people to begin walking in truth in smaller groups before the world does, so that the world will want to "taste and see that the LORD is good" (Psalm 34:8). In other words, the world will believe that God has sent Jesus.

As we seek God for solutions to help us explore the beauty of unity in diversity, in our own lives and in our churches, we will be tempted to be drawn toward programs. But I do not think God's answers will be found in ready-made solutions. We have to ask God to lead us in our own contexts in order to find the missing aspects of His presence among us.

If we maintain the vision of unity in diversity from His very heart, it will be enough to proceed in faith in order to accomplish His will.

For some churches this will mean a deliberate focus on bringing in people different from themselves. For others it may mean that their next pastor will be a different color from that of most of the congregation. For still others it could mean blending two or more congregations that have different ethnic makeup. All our efforts must begin with sincere relationships. God speaks to us through relationship. In the same manner of relationship, we can learn to love each other.

The ultimate relationships God has in mind reach far beyond mere partnerships. He wants spiritual *bonding* of all the diverse entities as we walk down the road together with joined hands. This kind of intimate partnership will be awkward at first; and as we enter this season of reconciliation, it will be important for whites, especially, to remember that for many minority peoples, the wounds are still raw.

Host peoples, for their part, must realize that forgiveness is essential in order to restore harmony and balance in our lands, so that our children can live in a world that honors and glorifies the Creator. For all host peoples, the issue of land will always be counted a factor in forgiveness. In most cases we have little or none of our original homelands. Now that the immigrants have most of them, perhaps some of our homelands can be returned, especially our sacred sites. Only God knows whether we will ever see this happen, but regardless, this takes a lot of forgiveness by host peoples. Such forgiveness can be applied only through the One who did nothing wrong but who has forgiven everything—Jesus Christ.

What Will It Take?

One of the more popular stories told in Cherokee country is called "Yonder Mountain." They say an old chief who had led his village to many victories in battle was about to step down. He had also provided protection and managed the food for his people in spite of hard times. Now it was time for him to pick a new chief.

189

He decided he would put the three leading men of the village to a test in order to determine who would be the best chief for the people. So the chief told the men to look out at yonder mountain. He told them they should go to the top of the mountain and bring back what they found.

Days went by. Finally the first man returned and reported to the old chief.

"On the way up the mountain," said the man, "I found these precious stones. With these stones we will have great trading power, and our people will never go hungry again. Here are just a few of these stones."

The chief looked at the stones and commended him for his shrewd thinking.

"You have done well," said the chief. "Now we will wait for the other men."

Several more days passed before the second man returned. Like the first, he had seen the precious stones but decided to pass them up. Before he reached the top of the mountain, just off the trail, the man found an abundant supply of medicinal plants and herbs. *With these herbs,* he had thought to himself, *our people will never have to suffer again.* He reported all these things to the chief and showed him a handful of the herbs.

"You have done well," said the chief, and commended him for his compassion for his people. "Now we must wait for the third man to return."

Several more days went by, and still the third man had not returned. The chief told the people that they would wait one more day. The next day the third man came stumbling in, worn out and exhausted. He explained to the chief what had happened.

"On the way up the mountain," he said, "I saw many precious stones, but I remembered that you said to go to the top of the mountain before returning, so I continued on. As I was getting a little closer to the top, I noticed just off the path more herbs and medicinal plants than I had ever seen. I knew our people could use these also, like the precious stones— but again I remembered that you said to go to the top of the mountain."

The young man continued, "The last part of the climb was the hardest, but I kept going until I reached the top of yonder mountain. Then, as I was resting, I saw smoke coming from a village down below. I could hear the people crying and I saw that they were in distress, so I climbed down the other side of the mountain. The people in this village were very poor and sick from hunger, but they had no medicine or valuable items to trade for food. I knew then what I needed to do.

"I climbed back up yonder mountain and started down the steep rocks. Then I found the trail and followed it until I came back to the medicine plants and herbs. I gathered up as many as I could. Then I went down further and filled my pouch with most of the precious stones, and I made my way back over the mountain to the village.

"It took a while for the people to recover with the herbs, so I took the precious stones downriver to the next village and traded them for food. The people of the village were finally beginning to recover, when I felt I should return to tell you these things. I have nothing now in my hands to show for the journey, but I felt I had no other choice, given the circumstances."

The old man took off his chief's robe and placed it on the back of the young man who came in last.

"You are the new chief," said the old man. "You have shown that you are able to see beyond the mountain, that there are people other than our own in need."

Jesus left His village in heaven, came to earth and went all the way to the top of the mountain where He found a cross. From there He looked down and saw beyond that mountain to our villages. We were dying, but He died in our place and saved us. He was made the Great High Chief and will reign forever. God is now calling His Church to see beyond our own villages and to recognize how much we need each other, so we can embrace His village in all its great diversity.

Wado . . . live in color!

Notes

Chapter 1: Uncovering the Myth of Sameness

1. Edwin S. Gaustad, ed., *A Documentary History of Religion in America to the Civil War* (Grand Rapids: Eerdmans, 1982), p. 129.

2. Ibid., p. 114.

3. Clyde Ellis, *To Change Them Forever: Indian Education at the Rainy Mountain Boarding School, 1893–1920* (Norman, Okla.: University of Oklahoma Press, 1996), p. 9.

4. Adrian Jacobs, *Pagan Prophets and Heathen Believers* (Rapid City, S.D.: self-published, 1999), p. 12.

5. Littleton Community Network-Biographies website: <www.littleton.org/LCN/governme/MUSEUM/history/PM16.htm>.

6. Russell Thornton, *American Indian Holocaust and Survival: A Population History Since 1492* (Norman, Okla.: University of Oklahoma Press, 1987), p. 32.

7. Ibid., p. 160.

8. Ibid., as quoted in the front matter.

9. Azusa Street Online website: <www.dunamai.com/brightspot/azusa. html>.

10. Christian Historical Preservation Society website: <www.christian-history.org/parham.html>.

11. Rick Joyner, *Azusa Street: The Fire That Could Not Die*, Christian Word website: <www.christianword.org/revival/fire/html>.

12. It should be noted that many of the Pentecostal denominations formed as a direct result of the Azusa Street revival came together in Memphis in October 1994 in an effort to put their racist roots behind them.

Chapter 2: The Origins of Unity in Diversity

1. For a discussion of the Hebrew words used here, including *Elohim*, see W. A. Pratney, *The Nature and Character of God: The Magnificent Doctrine of God in Understandable Language* (Minneapolis: Bethany, 1988), pp. 255–287.

Chapter 3: Choosing Jesus Over Cultural Christianity

1. R. Pierce Beaver, *Introduction to Native American Church History* (Tempe, Ariz.: Cook Christian Training School, 1983), p. 49.

2. Robert Antoine, quoted in Paul G. Hiebert, R. Daniel Shaw and Tite Tiénou, *Understanding Folk Religion: A Christian Response to Popular Beliefs and Practices* (Grand Rapids: Baker, 1999), p. 258.

3. Ibid., p. 293.

4. The word *Grandfather* is a respectful term some traditional Native Americans use for God.

Chapter 5: Romans and Galatians: Case Studies in Multicultural Conflict

1. W. Wiefel, "The Place of Origins of Romans," *Journal of Biblical Literature* 67 (1948), pp. 281–295.

2. James C. Walters, *Ethnic Issues in Paul's Letter to the Romans: Changing Self-Definition in Earliest Roman Christianity* (Valley Forge, Pa.: Trinity, 1993), p. 60.

Chapter 6: How Big Is Your God?

1. This story was told to me personally by Kiowa elders with firsthand knowledge of these events. It can also be found in the book by Isabel Crawford, *Joyful Journey* (Philadelphia: Judson, 1951).

2. Gaustad, *Documentary*, p. 84.

3. Ibid., p. 85.

4. Don Richardson, quoted in Ralph D. Winter, Steven C. Hawthorne, eds., *Perspectives on the World Christian Movement: A Reader* (Pasadena, Calif.: William Carey Library, 1981), p. 416.

5. Dr. Suuqiina, *Maniilaq: An Eskimo Prophet* (Anchor Point, Alaska: self-published, 2001), p. 22.

6. Douglas McMurry, *The Discoverers* (Richmond, Va.: work in progress).

7. Stan Hoig, *Peace Chiefs of the Cheyennes* (Oklahoma City: University of Oklahoma Press, 1980), p. 7.

8. Jacobs, *Pagan*, pp. 6–9.

9. It is illegal for anyone in the United States to kill an eagle. Native Americans affiliated with federally recognized tribes can apply for eagle feathers and carcasses. It usually takes about three years to obtain them.

Chapter 7: Race and Cultures Clash: Our Wake-Up Call

1. This report was prepared by Wan He and Frank Hobbs of the U.S. Census Bureau and funded by the Minority Business Development Agency, U.S. Department of Commerce.

Chapter 8: The Subtleties of Racism

1. The discussion on Britain's history is taken from *Australian Reminiscences and Papers of L. E. Threlkeld (Missionary to the Aborigines 1824–1859)*, Niel Gunson, ed. (Australian Institute of Aboriginal Studies, 1974), pp. 148–149.

2. "Britons Discover Heritage Is Not So Black and White," *New Zealand Herald*, Telegraph Group, London (November 10, 1999).

Chapter 9: Exposing the Original Oppressor

1. "Documentary Genocide," *The Richmond Times-Dispatch* (Sunday, March 5, 2000), p. 1.

2. Ibid. Discussion on this subject can also be found under "Seeking Sovereignty," *The Richmond Times-Dispatch* (Monday, March 6, 2000), p. 1.

3. Caplan, 1992, quoted in Center for Bioethics Virtual Library website: <www.med.upenn.edu/~bioethic/library/papers/art/EugenicsNotreDame.html>.

4. "Bad Blood: The Troubling Legacy of the Tuskegee Syphilis Study," University of Virginia Health Systems, Historical Collections website: <www.med.virginia.edu/hs-library/historical/apology/index.html>.

5. Proctor, 1988, quoted in Center for Bioethics website (see endnote #3).

6. See Africa2000 website: <www.africa2000.com/ENDX/ aepage.htm>.

7. Lisa M. Koonan and Jack C. Smith, "Legal, Induced Abortion, Reproductive Health of Women," Centers for Disease Control and Prevention website: <www.cdc.gov/nccdphp/drh/datoct/pdf/rhow6.pdf>.

8. See Africa2000 (endnote #6).

9. Jim Sedlak, Public Policy Director at The American Life League, Inc., in a phone conversation with me on December 15, 2000.

Chapter 10: Honorable Mention: The Good Guys

1. Beaver, *Introduction*, pp. 35– 36.
2. C. A. Weslager, *The Delaware Indians: A History* (New Brunswick, N.J.: Rutgers University Press, 1972), p. 166, quoted in Darrell Fields, *The Seed of a Nation: Reconciling with the Birth of America* (Mechanicsburg, Pa.: Covenant, 2000), p. 62.
3. Samuel M. Janney, *The Life of William Penn* (Philadelphia: Friends' Book Association, 1851), p. 214, quoted in Fields, *Seed*, p. 63.
4. C. Hale Sipe, *The Indian Wars of Pennsylvania* (Lewisburg, Pa.: Wennawoods, 1995), p. 71, quoted in Fields, *Seed*, p. 64.
5. The description of these events was taken from the Early America Review website: <www.earlyamerica.com/review/fall96/johnson.html>.
6. The information for this section was gained through the author's original research in the Evan Jones Collection at the Valley Forge, Pa., American Baptist Historical Society, 1988–89. The fifteen boxes of journals and letters are not marked.
7. These events taken from Beaver, *Introduction*, pp. 72–73, and from oral tradition.
8. This story was told to me personally by Kiowa elders with firsthand knowledge of these events. It can also be found in Crawford, *Journey*.

Chapter 13: Protocol: Relating to God, His People and His Land

1. Dr. Suuqiina, *Can You Feel the Mountains Tremble? A Healing the Land Handbook* (Anchorage, Alaska: Inuit Ministry International, 1999), pp. 77–78.
2. Ibid., pp. 45–63.
3. Samuel Cole Williams, *Adair's History of the American Indians* (Johnson City, Tenn.: Watauga, 1930), pp. 244–245.
4. Charles Hamilton, ed., *Cry of the Thunderbird: The American Indian's Own Story* (Norman, Okla.: University of Oklahoma Press, 1989), p. 238.
5. Winkie Pratney, *Healing the Land: A Supernatural View of Ecology* (Grand Rapids: Chosen, 1993), p. 142.
6. Suuqiina, *Can You Feel*, p. 40.

Chapter 14: Getting Beyond "Getting Along"

1. John Dawson, *Healing America's Wounds* (Ventura, Calif.: Regal, 1994), pp. 77–78.
2. Stephen Carter, *The Culture of Disbelief: How American Law and Politics Trivialize Religious Devotion* (New York: Basic, 1993), pp. 14–15.

Chapter 15: What Does the Kingdom Look Like?

1. Mark Matthews, "Montana Tribe Takes the Road Less Traveled," *Writers on the Range* (P.O. Box 1090, Peoria, CO 81428), March 7, 2001.

Annotated Bibliography

I wanted to write a book that was readable to adults at all levels, yet one that was not simplistic—a book that challenged the modern American Church culture to rethink how it deals with Jesus Christ. I wanted to write a book that allowed non–Native Americans to see another side of us and thereby see another part of themselves. In this spirit I offer a short annotated bibliography for those who would like to read more.

Several books describe the American dilemma we now face. Here is the current textbook for finding a vision of what America can be and a path toward America's godly future:

Dawson, John. *Healing America's Wounds*. Ventura, Calif.: Regal, 1994.

Another vision that concentrates largely on white-Indian relations is:

Fields, Darrell. *The Seed of a Nation: Reconciling with the Birth of America*. Mechanicsburg, Pa.: Covenant, 2000.

For a good lesson in American history from a perspective you may have missed in school, read:

Loewen, James W. *Lies My Teacher Told Me: Everything Your American History Textbook Got Wrong*. New York: Touchstone, 1995.

For specific Native American references along these lines:

Churchill, Ward. *A Little Matter of Genocide: Holocaust and Denial in the Americas, 1492 to the Present*. San Francisco: City Light, 1997.

Three books offer a historic view of how religion has affected American culture:

Dayton, Donald. *Discovering an Evangelical Heritage*. Peabody, Mass.: Hendrickson, 1976.

Lovelace, Richard F. *Dynamics of a Spiritual Life: An Evangelical Theology of Renewal.* Downers Grove, Ill.: InterVarsity, 1979.

McLoughlin, William. *Revivals, Awakenings, and Reform.* Chicago: University of Chicago, 1978.

For a more current political take on the issues, see:

Carter, Stephen L. *The Culture of Disbelief: How American Law and Politics Trivialize Religious Devotion.* New York: Basic, 1993.

For a great understanding of how religious, cultural and other oppression is perpetuated, read:

Freire, Paulo. *Pedagogy of the Oppressed.* New York: Continuum, 1997.

Two biblical theologies for word studies and other references are:

Moody, Dale. *The Word of Truth: A Summary of Christian Doctrine Based on Biblical Revelation.* Grand Rapids: Eerdmans, 1981.

Pratney, W. A. *The Nature and Character of God: The Magnificent Doctrine of God in Understandable Language.* Minneapolis: Bethany, 1988.

A good commentary for biblical background is:

Keener, Craig S. *The IVP Bible Background Commentary.* Downers Grove, Ill.: InterVarsity, 1993.

Understanding the apostle Paul, his background and culture is a key to developing a better church theology. A classic and more scholarly text is:

Davies, W. D. *Paul and Rabbinic Judaism: Some Rabbinic Elements in Pauline Theology.* London, SPCK, 1965.

A more concise, easier read is:

Walters, James C. *Ethnic Issues in Paul's Letter to the Romans: Changing Self-Definitions in Earliest Roman Christianity.* Valley Forge, Pa.: Trinity, 1993.

As important as it is to know where we have been, it is also helpful to find out where we are going. Many books could be recommended on the Church, but all are missing one element or another. I offer two, one old and one new, that give a fuller picture from two unique vantage points, although neither deals with ethnic issues, per se. The classic oldie has more meat than you can chew, and the newer one has a good view of a near-comprehensive Gospel:

197

Bonhoeffer, Dietrich. *Life Together: A Discussion of Christian Fellowship*. San Francisco: Harper & Row, 1954.

Sider, Ronald J. *Good News and Good Works: A Theology for the Whole Gospel*. Grand Rapids: Baker, 1993.

A number of worthwhile missiology books and compilations have been released in the past few decades. I will mention only four, going from the thinnest to the thickest:

Inch, Morris A. *Doing Theology Across Cultures*. Grand Rapids: Baker, 1982.

Hiebert, Paul G. *Anthropological Reflections on Missiological Issues*. Grand Rapids: Baker, 1994.

Hiebert, Paul G., Daniel R. Shaw and Tite Tiénou. *Understanding Folk Religion: A Christian Response to Popular Beliefs and Practices*. Grand Rapids: Baker, 1999.

Winter, Ralph, and Steven C. Hawthorne, eds. *Perspectives on the World Christian Movement: A Reader*. Pasadena: William Carey Library, 1992.

A key to understanding my book, and the role of the Church in the world as well, is grasping the theology of natural revelation. There are three books with more personal flavor that I consider absolute reading:

Lewis, C. S. *The Abolition of Man: How Education Develops Man's Sense of Morality*. New York: Macmillan, 1947.

Richardson, Don. *Eternity in Their Hearts: The Untold Story of Christianity Among Folk Religions of Ancient People*. Ventura, Calif.: Regal, 1981.

Olson, Bruce. *Bruchko*. Orlando: Creation House, 1995.

Concerning race and ethnic issues, the majority of books by far focuses on white/black relations. Good points of discussion can be gleaned from these books relevant to all races and ethnicities. Three I recommend to further this dialogue are:

Page, Clarence. *Showing My Color: Impolite Essays on Race and Identity*. New York: Harper Perennial, 1996.

Perkins, Spencer, and Chris Rice. *More Than Equals: Racial Healing for the Sake of the Gospel*. Downers Grove, Ill.: InterVarsity, 1993.

Usry, Glenn, and Craig S. Keener. *Black Man's Religion: Can Christianity Be Afrocentric?* Downers Grove, Ill.: InterVarsity, 1996.

A book that will help you understand the vast differences in worldviews between the dominant American society and Native Americans is:

Mander, Jerry. *In the Absence of the Sacred: The Failure of Technology and the Survival of the Indian Nations.* San Francisco: Sierra Club, 1991.

Two helpful books in the same area are written from a Christian perspective:

Jacobs, Adrian. *Aboriginal Christianity: The Way It Was Meant to Be.* Rapid City, S.D.: self-published, 1998.

Twiss, Richard. *One Church, Many Tribes: Following Jesus the Way God Made You.* Ventura, Calif.: Regal, 2000.

Concerning racial reconciliation, refer to John Dawson's *Healing America's Wounds* as listed above.

Three books are recommended for understanding the issues surrounding healing the land. They are:

Campolo, Tony. *How to Rescue the Earth without Worshiping Nature: A Christian's Call to Save Creation.* Nashville: Thomas Nelson, 1992.

Pratney, Winkie. *Healing the Land: A Supernatural View of Ecology.* Grand Rapids: Chosen, 1993.

Suuqiina. *Can You Feel the Mountains Tremble? A Healing the Land Handbook.* Anchorage, Alaska: Inuit Ministry International, 1999.

Especially recommended for those who need more perspective on listening:

Tournier, Paul. *A Listening Ear: Reflections on Christian Caring.* Minneapolis: Augsburg, 1986.

Index

203

Randy Woodley, who earned an M.Div. from Eastern Baptist Theological Seminary, is a Keetoowah Cherokee Indian who has been in ministry among Native Americans for nearly two decades. He uses his unique cultural heritage to reach traditional Native Americans with the Gospel.

Randy is president and co-founder with his wife, Edith (Eastern Shoshone/Choctaw), of Eagle's Wings Ministry, a ministry of Native American believers reaching Native Americans and others with the good news of Jesus Christ through Native culture. Together the Woodleys utilize Bible teaching, preaching, reconciliation, song, dance, ceremony, drama and other means to minister God's love to a people who rarely receive it through the attempts of the modern Church. They are forerunners in the current move of God in what is being called the Native American Contextual Movement.

Randy is the former pastor of the Eagle Valley Church in Carson City, Nevada, a fellowship that expresses worship and ministry using its own Native culture, and that has served for years as a unique role model of an authentic Native American Christian church.

Randy's training and experience regarding racial, ethnic, cultural and religious diversity are extensive, and he has become a noted teacher on these issues. He is also recognized as a leader within the International Reconciliation Movement and its host network, A.D. 2000 & Beyond. His is a welcome and necessary prophetic teaching voice in the Church.

Randy and Edith are in the process of founding the Southeast Native American Ministry, Conference and Culture Center in western North Carolina. The Center will train Native American ministry leaders to take the Gospel back to their own reservations and towns in a culturally relevant way.

The Woodleys have four children and currently reside in Alabama.

For further information contact:

Eagle's Wings Ministry
1580 Marvin Adcock Rd.
Hayden, AL 35079
Web address: www.eagles-wingsmin.com
e-mail at: rw@eagles-wingsmin.com